The Amazing Acid Alkaline Cookbook

The Amazing Acid Alkaline Cookbook

Balancing Taste, Nutrition, and Your pH Levels

Bonnie Ross

FOREWORD BY DR. SUSAN E. BROWN

SQUAREONE
PUBLISHERS

COVER DESIGNER: Jeannie Tudor
EDITOR: Michael Weatherhead
TYPESETTER: Gary A. Rosenberg

Square One Publishers
115 Herricks Road
Garden City Park, NY 11040
(516) 535-2010 • (877) 900-BOOK
www.squareonepublishers.com

Library of Congress Cataloging-in-Publication Data

Ross, Bonnie, 1956-
  The amazing acid alkaline cookbook : balancing taste, nutrition, and your pH levels / Bonnie Ross.
      p. cm.
  Includes index.
  ISBN 978-0-7570-0316-5
  1. Acid-base imbalances—Diet therapy. 2. Acid-base imbalances—Nutritional
aspects. 3. Acid-base equilibrium—Health aspects. 4.
Cookbooks. I. Title.
  RC630.R69 2011
  641.5'631--dc22

                                      2010045020

The food listings found on pages 9 through 13 are reprinted from
The Acid-Alkaline Food Guide, copyright © 2006 by Susan E. Brown
and Larry Trivieri, Jr. Reprinted by permission.

Printed in the United States of America

10   9   8   7   6   5

CONTENTS

Appendix

*This book is dedicated to
Rose Featherstone, for the spark.*

FOREWORD

At the age of 102 my beloved grandmother died of complications after a hip fracture. I could not help but wonder how long she might have lived had that fracture been avoided. Her death sparked an intense desire in me to understand the true nature, causes, preventative measures, and treatment of osteoporosis. I hoped that by identifying all of the factors at play in this degenerative process, I could develop a program that would stop it from debilitating others. What I found was both startling and encouraging. Through exhaustive research, I discovered that bone strength is maintained not only through exercise and the intake of at least twenty key bone-building nutrients but also by keeping the body in a state of optimum acid-alkaline (pH) balance. While mainstream medical thought had been focused on using medications to interfere with the process of bone loss, little attention had been given to how bone loss could be avoided in the first place. By teaching the importance of proper pH balance in bone health, I knew that the number of osteoporosis victims could be reduced through a change in the most vital lifestyle choice you can

make: your diet. Further, the more I learned about pH balance, the more I recognized its potential to stop a number of other serious illnesses in their tracks. My years of research culminated in the writing of my first book, Better Bones, Better Body; followed by my second book, *The Acid-Alkaline Food Guide.*

Over the nearly two decades of teaching my bone-preserving Alkaline for Life® program, hundreds of people have asked me to write or find them a cookbook that would help them eat the acid-alkaline way. It is with great pleasure that I can now recommend Bonnie Ross's groundbreaking work *The Amazing Acid-Alkaline Cookbook.* I am happy to say that Bonnie's cookbook nicely complements the work to which I have dedicated much of my life. The Amazing Acid-Alkaline Cookbook is a comprehensive collection of recipes that will have your taste buds singing while bringing your body back to its natural state of equilibrium. The best part is that there is nothing lacking in the book. In it you will find recipes not only for flavorful main dishes and sides but also for delicious pancakes, biscuits, cookies, muffins, cakes, and pies. They are all here for you to enjoy. And that may be the best thing about this cookbook (aside from the Carrot Pineapple Cake with Cream Cheese Frosting): It eases you into a lifestyle change that can really change your life. In addition to creating wonderful meals, this book also explains the common ingredients used in acid-alkaline cooking and points you towards a few helpful pieces of kitchen equipment that can get you started on the right foot. And if all that weren't enough, you will find interesting bits of information on the subject of pH sprinkled throughout.

Much as I was driven to learn about pH balance by my grandmother's passing, Bonnie was compelled to discover the acid-alkaline lifestyle by the death of not only her high school sweetheart, but also her brother. I suppose loss has put us both on a mission to see that your health remains vibrant, strong, and free of preventable illness. It is a source of fulfillment for me that my work provided a solid basis for Bonnie to follow her inspiration and write this cookbook. So eat well, be healthy, live happily, and share this information with others over a delicious pH-balanced dinner.

Susan E. Brown, Ph.D.
Author of *Better Bones, Better Body;*
and *The Acid-Alkaline Food Guide*
Director of the Better Bones Foundation
www.betterbones.com

PREFACE

Two years ago, while catching up with my long-time friend Rose, I heard the sad news that my high school sweetheart, Rod, had been stricken with cancer and that the prognosis was not good. Rose then told me about a book she had read about the importance of balancing the pH level of your body. According to the book, following a pH-balanced diet could help fight the proliferation of cancer cells, not to mention aid in the avoidance of a long list of other health issues. Rose wanted to share the information with Rod, but he had already left on a long last trip to do and see the things he had always wanted to do and see.

I, however, was very curious about her findings, as my little brother had recently died of a rare blood cancer that was considered even more uncommon due to his young age. I had a very good idea of his diet, which had always concerned me. I wanted to compare his diet with the foods listed in the book Rose had mentioned. I ordered everything I could find on pH balance from the library and started researching the subject online as well.

A light bulb went on in my head. It turned out that just about everything my brother ate was acid-forming. Upon reviewing our own diet, my husband and I were absolutely shocked to discover how much acidifying food we consumed on a daily basis. We had thought we laid a pretty healthy table. We were wrong.

After reading all of the information I could get my hands on regarding pH balance, I came to the conclusion that my family had to change the food we were putting in our bodies. I wanted to protect my family from illness and knew that the best way to do so would be through diet.

Two problems immediately came to the surface. The first one was the many and varied lists of acid-alkaline foods that I had found. Each list seemed to have different opinions concerning what was acidifying and what was alkalizing. It was very confusing. Finally, I came across a no-nonsense list of acid-alkaline foods that had the research and science to back it up. That book was *The Acid-Alkaline Food Guide* by nutritionist Dr. Susan Brown and Larry Trivieri, Jr. It gave me the foundation for a new way of eating. I relied heavily on its data during the creation of these recipes.

The second problem was not so easy to solve. Unfortunately, most of the recipes found in the other acid-alkaline books I had come across were unappealing, unimaginative, or too far off from the meals that the average home cook, such as I, would attempt. I wanted familiar menus and old-fashioned North American dishes that would not seem at all out of place in my grandparents' kitchen, albeit prepared with a few different ingredients. Apparently, if my family was going to eat more pH-balanced meals, I would have to create them on my own.

Thankfully, with the help of *The Acid-Alkaline Food Guide,* I was able to develop a variety of alkalizing courses that were not only nutritionally sound, but also satisfying, delicious, and easy to make. We were amazed by the almost immediate effects the new diet had on us. Weight began to come off easily. Gone was that familiar sluggish feeling after eating. I even noticed improvements in our energy levels. Within only a few weeks, my family felt better prepared to fight off and prevent disease. We began to sleep more soundly and had less pain from arthritic joints.

After several months of following the diet, my husband and I spent a week over the holidays reverting to our old habits of eating primarily acid-forming foods. In no time, we felt our energy levels drop and experienced significant joint pain. We became bloated and uncomfortable. We soon rededicated ourselves to the pH-balanced lifestyle, and within a week were fully recovered. All was well again. The experience was a lesson learned but not to be repeated.

Having realized the value of this new way of eating, I started sharing my pH-balanced recipes with my friends and extended family, and they were a hit. It wasn't long before my husband said those five little words every part-time chef secretly longs to hear: "You should write a cookbook!" So I did.

INTRODUCTION

Prepare to be amazed by the effects a pH-balanced diet can have on your body. You will feel the difference almost immediately. By using the recipes in this cookbook on a daily basis, not only will you be more energetic and alert, you will also help to protect yourself and your family from illness and disease. And while this book is not a weight-loss routine, if you adhere to its principles and show a little restraint with dessert portions, you will eventually achieve your healthy normal body weight with less effort than you ever imagined. To assist you further in that goal, many of the recipes in this book are pH-balanced versions of meals commonly considered "comfort foods," which should alleviate the sense of denial that diets so often trigger.

Although this is not a vegetarian cookbook, it contains numerous hearty vegetable and grain meals that have all the protein your body requires. Those dishes that include meat and dairy have been adapted to be more alkaline, often by merely adjusting the ratio of meat and dairy to vegetables and grains. You will soon find that a family of five can get all the nutrition they need by sharing two chicken breasts and enjoying a satisfying serving of vegetables and grains, instead of having the meat take center stage on the plate.

Many of the recipes in this book are yeast-free and wheat-free, which not only cuts their acidity, but also is a blessing to those with certain dietary restrictions. But I assure you, the baked goods will thoroughly please any sweet tooth.

From quick breakfasts to leisurely weekend brunches, be it a fast family meal or an elegant dinner party, this cookbook covers every occasion. Remarkably easy to prepare, these dishes have been designed with busy schedules in mind and can be made in bulk to be eaten throughout the week. So don't wait a second longer to change your life. *The Amazing Acid-Alkaline Cookbook* is here to get your health on track through nutritious pH-balanced eating.

Happy cooking!

PART ONE

The pH-Balanced Lifestyle

1. What Is pH?

More and more each day, people are looking not only for ways to cure illness and disease but also for ways to *prevent* illness and disease from occurring in the first place. While doctors and hospitals are doing their best to place themselves at the cutting edge of medicine, they are still treating a problem once it has *become* a problem. We are all slowly starting to realize that the best and most effective "cure" is to stop that problem *before* it takes hold.

But how can the average person possibly hope to avoid what feels like the unavoidable? What chance do we stand in the face of cancer, cardiovascular disease, arthritis, diabetes, kidney disease, osteoporosis, premature aging, or even the most common everyday allergies?

Fortunately, the solution lies right in front of our noses—well, mouths. It is sitting there on the end of our forks. It is—plain and simple—the food we eat. Your food choices are the first and most powerful line of defense against illness. The real problem is that our modern diet has shifted the body out of balance, tipping the scales towards a highly acidic—and thus, highly dis-

ease-promoting—way of life. Thankfully, we can tip them back, regaining our equilibrium and our health. The first step towards this goal is to understand pH.

UNDERSTANDING pH

While this is most certainly a cookbook and not a science textbook, the principles behind each delicious recipe are definitely scientific, and deserve a little explanation.

The term pH stands for "potential for hydrogen" and indicates the concentration of hydrogen ions in any particular solution. The pH scale measures whether a solution is acidic, alkaline, or neutral. That scale ranges from 0 to 14, with 0 to 6 being acidic, 7 being neutral, and 8 to14 being alkaline. In other words, the lower the pH number of a solution, the more acidic it is. Our bodies have evolved in such a way as to require a near-perfect balance of acids and alkaline bases in order to maintain optimum health. To understand pH, you must first understand the way your body metabolizes food.

Upon digestion, most foods are metabolized to contribute either hydrogen ions (which are acid-forming) or bicarbonate ions (which are alkalizing) to your system. Thus, when you speak of metabolic pH balance, you are speaking of the balance between these two food-derived substances. For example, the potassium citrate in fruit is metabolized into alkalizing potassium bicarbonate, while the sulfur-containing amino acids in protein are metabolized into acidifying sulfuric acid residue.

The more hydrogen ions are released from a food, the more acidic your system will become. Thankfully, the more alkalizing foods we consume, the more we are able to neutralize this acidity. Of course, you need both acid-forming and alkaline-forming foods for good health, but you need them in balance. Unfortunately, most of us consume far too many acid-forming foods, such as meat and sugar, and far too few alka-line-forming foods, such as fruit and vegetables. It is a way of life that tilts your body towards acidity, which can deplete your bones of important minerals, increase your risk of kidney stones, weaken your immunity, and limit your overall health.

MEASURING YOUR PH BALANCE

While it is no easy task to determine your body's overall pH level exactly, you can use pH test strips to gauge the acidity of your urine or saliva. Available at most pharmacies and online (see the Resources section on page 149), pH test strips indicate different pH values by turning different colors after coming into contact with a fluid. The best way to measure your body's pH on your own is to urinate onto a test strip first thing in the morning, particularly after six hours of rest with-

pH Numbers

It may seem confusing that a *lower* pH number value actually refers to a *higher* level of acidity. But, there's a method to the madness. The 0 to 14 scale is actually shorthand for the *true* representation of a solution's concentration of hydrogen ions, which is calculated using a negative logarithm and expressed in moles per liter. For example, purified water, which is generally neutral, has a pH of 0.0000001 moles per liter. We shorten that by expressing the value as a power of 10. Thus, purified water has a pH of 10 to the power of -7, or 10^{-7}. We then shorten that further by dropping the 10 and the minus sign, and simply use the number 7.

A more acidic solution would have a higher concentration of hydrogen ions, and thus the pH value would be closer to a whole number. For example, an extremely acidic solution might have a pH of 0.01, or 10^{-2}. Our shorthand would then express that value as a pH of 2. Conversely, the more alkaline a solution, the farther away its pH value would be from a whole number (as we see with purified water)—in other words, the further the solution is from being *completely* acidic. So, something even more alkaline than water might have a pH of 0.000000001, or 10^{-9}, or simply 9.

out urination. Morning urine will offer a good indication of the acid your body has been eliminating throughout the night. (Please note, any medication taken before bed may affect your pH reading.) The ideal pH for morning urine ranges from 6.5 to 7.5.

As an optional method, you may test your morning saliva. (It is important, however, that you not eat, drink, or brush your teeth before you test your saliva's pH.) Put a small amount of saliva onto a plastic spoon and dip the test paper into the saliva. Be aware that the number considered normal for a saliva reading is not the same as the normal range for a urine test. The target reading for saliva falls between 6.0 and 7.5.

pH AND HEALTH

Normally, acids are buffered by the bases in the foods you eat as well as certain neutralizing compounds in your system. Unfortunately, the majority of the foods eaten in the typical North American diet are mainly acid-forming, putting your body in a constant struggle to neutralize that acid in an effort to return itself to its slightly alkaline ideal. In time, a consistent diet of overly acid-forming foods will result in excess acidity, which begins to accumulate in your tissues. Before you know it, your body is in a state of low-grade metabolic acidosis. And this is where the problems start.

In the absence of alkalizing foods, the body attempts to restore its preferred alkaline balance by drawing on, and possibly depleting, its own vital reserves of alkalizing minerals. When your body takes these compounds, which include calcium and magnesium, from your bones and teeth, the loss can lead to osteoporosis and gum disease. Low-grade metabolic acidosis also causes increased inflammation and degeneration of connective tissue, resulting in symptoms of osteoarthritis, rheumatoid arthritis, gout, and fibromyalgia. Many other disorders, including cardiovascular disease, obesity, diabetes, bladder and kidney conditions, immune deficiency, eczema, cellulitis, low energy, chronic fatigue, and even some forms of cancer have been linked to high levels of acid in the body. On the other hand, research has shown that cancer cells do not thrive as successfully in an alkaline environment.

By cutting back on acidifying foods—such as meat, dairy products, and coffee—as well as eating more alkalizing foods—such as vegetables and fruit—you will be able to reduce the burden of metabolic acidosis in your system and recover lost minerals. This does not mean, however, that you should eliminate acid-forming foods entirely from your diet. If you are suffering extreme acidosis, a few days of eating strictly alkalizing food choices will give you a good start towards balancing your pH level. An exclusively alkaline diet for more than a few days, however, is not recommended, as your body needs the protein, vitamins, minerals, and essential fatty acids that some of the more acidifying foods provide. Along with proper fluid intake and regular exercise, moderation of acid-forming foods is the key to proper pH balance. If you are in good health, 60 to 65 percent of each meal you eat should be alkalizing, and of course, all of it should be nutritious.

You may find it helpful to keep a journal of your pH results over the first few weeks or months of eating an acid-alkaline balanced diet.

You will see an actual change in your level of acidity and know that you're improving your health. You will also notice an increase in your energy level as your body becomes more alkaline.

pH BALANCE
AND WEIGHT LOSS

Remember that the achievement of a healthy pH level should be attempted at every meal. An all-alkaline dinner will not make up for an acid-forming diet throughout the day, just as binging on alkalizing foods over the entire weekend will not make up for a week's worth of acidifying foods in your system. Eating only meat at every meal may help you lose some short-term weight, but the resulting acid waste build-up is sure to cause health problems in the long term. Try having an alkalizing salad or vegetable dish as your main dish and complement it with a small serving of meat, if necessary. Also, enjoy fruit rather than a heavy dessert after the meal to satisfy your sweet tooth. You don't even need to worry about portion control when eating fruit and vegetables. Just be sure to keep them simple, avoiding all of the unhealthy toppings that can turn a nutritious snack into a damaging one. By cutting out the processed foods and increasing your vegetable intake, you will be able to lose weight and maintain a healthy pH balance.

APPEARANCE
VERSUS EFFECT

It is important to note the difference between the appearance of acidity in a food and that food's effect on your acid-alkaline balance. For example, lemons are commonly known for their sourness, which is caused by the citric acid they contain. Once digested, however, lemons actually have an alkalizing effect on your body, as their citric acid is metabolized into bicarbonate. Similarly, meat may seem alkaline before digestion, but its high level of protein actually leaves a residue of sulfuric acid in your body once it has been metabolized. Keep this idea in mind when you see the list of foods below and glance through the recipes presented in later chapters.

FOOD TABLES

The following tables divide common foods into nine categories, including fruits; vegetables; legumes; animal products; grains, nuts, and seeds; seasonings; oils and butters; beverages; and "other." For each food, you will learn whether it has a medium-to-high alkalizing effect, a low-to-medium alkalizing effect, a low-to-medium acidifying effect, or a medium-to-high acidifying effect. If you use only the recipes in this book to compose your meals, you will not have to check the following tables because you will know that each dish is pH-balanced. If you choose to use your own recipes some or much of the time, remember that 60 to 65 percent of your plate should contain foods from the alkalizing side of the table.

If you are trying to fight a particularly bad case of acidosis, you may want to up the percentage of alkalizing foods and further limit your consumption of acid-forming foods for a few days. Once your pH returns to a healthy level, you can resume following the ideal division of foods mentioned previously.

pH Values of Food

FOOD	ALKALIZING EFFECT		ACIDIFYING EFFECT	
	MEDIUM TO HIGH	LOW TO MEDIUM	LOW TO MEDIUM	MEDIUM TO HIGH
FRUIT				
Apple		■		
Apricot		■		
Banana		■		
Blackberry	■			
Blueberry		■		
Boysenberry		■		
Cantaloupe	■			
Cheriyoma			■	
Cherry		■		
Cranberry				■
Currant		■		
Date			■	
Fig		■		
Grape		■		
Grapefruit		■		
Guava			■	
Honey Dew Melon	■			
Kiwi	■			
Lemon		■		
Lime	■			
Mandarin Orange	■			
Mango	■			
Orange		■		
Papaya	■			
Peach		■		

FOOD	ALKALIZING EFFECT		ACIDIFYING EFFECT	
	MEDIUM TO HIGH	LOW TO MEDIUM	LOW TO MEDIUM	MEDIUM TO HIGH
Pear		■		
Persimmon	■			
Pineapple	■			
Plum			■	
Pomegranate				■
Prune			■	
Raisin (unsulfured)	■			
Raspberry		■		
Rhubarb			■	
Strawberry	■			
Tangelo		■		
Tangerine	■			
Tomato			■	
Watermelon	■			
VEGETABLES				
Agar		■		
Artichokes		■		
Asparagus	■			
Avocado	■			
Beets	■			
Black Olives				■
Broccoli		■		
Brussel Sprouts		■		
Burdock Root	■			
Cabbages		■		
Carrots (non-organic)			■	

FOOD	ALKALIZING EFFECT		ACIDIFYING EFFECT	
	MEDIUM TO HIGH	LOW TO MEDIUM	LOW TO MEDIUM	MEDIUM TO HIGH
Carrots (organic)		X		
Cauliflower		X		
Celery	X			
Cilantro		X		
Collard Greens	X			
Corn				X
Cucumber		X		
Daikon Radish	X			
Dandelion Greens		X		
Dill Weed		X		
Dulse	X			
Eggplant		X		
Endive	X			
Garlic		X		
Green Olives (in brine)	X			
Hijiki Seaweed	X			
Hubbard Squash		X		
Irish Moss		X		
Jerusalem Artichokes		X		
Jicama		X		
Kale	X			
Kelp	X			
Kohlrabi	X			
Kombu	X			
Lettuce		X		
Lotus Root	X			
Mushroom		X		
Mustard Greens	X			
Nori	X			
Okra		X		

FOOD	ALKALIZING EFFECT		ACIDIFYING EFFECT	
	MEDIUM TO HIGH	LOW TO MEDIUM	LOW TO MEDIUM	MEDIUM TO HIGH
Onion	X			
Parsnip	X			
Potato		X		
Radish	X			
Rutabaga	X			
Salad Greens		X		
Scallions		X		
Spinach			X	
Spirulina	X			
Sprouts		X		
Summer Squash		X		
Sweet Potato	X			
Swiss Chard			X	
Taro Root	X			
Turnip		X		
Turnip Greens		X		
Wakame	X			
Winter Squash		X		
Yams	X			
Zucchini		X		
LEGUMES				
Adzuki Beans				X
Black Beans				X
Chickpeas				X
Fava Beans				X
Great Northern Beans				X
Green Beans				X
Kidney Beans				X
Lentils			X	
Lima Beans			X	

FOOD	ALKALIZING EFFECT		ACIDIFYING EFFECT	
	MEDIUM TO HIGH	LOW TO MEDIUM	LOW TO MEDIUM	MEDIUM TO HIGH
Mung Beans			▓	
Navy Beans			▓	
Peas			▓	
Pinto Beans			▓	
Snow Peas		▓		
Soybean Curd (Tofu)				▓
Soybeans				▓
Soy Flour				▓
Soy Milk				▓
Soy Nuts				▓
Soy Protein				▓
Yellow Beans			▓	

ANIMAL PRODUCTS

FOOD	ALKALIZING EFFECT		ACIDIFYING EFFECT	
	MEDIUM TO HIGH	LOW TO MEDIUM	LOW TO MEDIUM	MEDIUM TO HIGH
Beef				▓
Butter			▓	
Cheese				▓
Clams			▓	
Cow's Milk			▓	
Cream			▓	
Cream Cheese			▓	
Curd Cheese			▓	
Egg Whites			▓	
Fish				▓
Goat				▓
Kefir			▓	
Lamb				▓
Shellfish (Except Clams)				▓
Pork				▓
Poultry				▓
Sour Cream			▓	

FOOD	ALKALIZING EFFECT		ACIDIFYING EFFECT	
	MEDIUM TO HIGH	LOW TO MEDIUM	LOW TO MEDIUM	MEDIUM TO HIGH
Whey (Cow or Goat)		▓		
Whole Eggs				▓
Wild Game				▓
Yogurt (Sweetened)				▓
Yogurt (Unsweetened)			▓	

GRAINS, NUTS, AND SEEDS

FOOD	ALKALIZING EFFECT		ACIDIFYING EFFECT	
	MEDIUM TO HIGH	LOW TO MEDIUM	LOW TO MEDIUM	MEDIUM TO HIGH
Almond Milk (Unsweetened)		▓		
Almonds		▓		
Amaranth Flour			▓	
Arborio Rice		▓		
Barley				▓
Barley Flour				▓
Basmati Rice		▓		
Brown Rice			▓	
Buckwheat				▓
Bulgur Wheat				▓
Cashews		▓		
Chestnuts	▓			
Coconuts			▓	
Couscous				▓
Farina				▓
Flaxseed		▓		
Grits				▓
Hazelnuts		▓		
Hops				
Japonica Rice		▓		
Kamut Flour			▓	
Macadamia Nuts		▓		
Malt				▓

FOOD	ALKALIZING EFFECT		ACIDIFYING EFFECT	
	MEDIUM TO HIGH	LOW TO MEDIUM	LOW TO MEDIUM	MEDIUM TO HIGH
Millet			■	
Oat Bran				■
Oat Flour		■		
Oatmeal (Unsweetened)			■	
Peanuts				■
Pecans				■
Pine Nuts			■	
Pistachios				■
Pumpkin Seeds	■			
Quinoa		■		
Rice Milk				■
Rye Flour				■
Sesame Seeds		■		
Spelt Flour			■	
Sunflower Seeds		■		
Teff			■	
Triticale			■	
Walnuts				■
Wheat (Unrefined)			■	
White Flour				■
White Flour Pasta				■
White Rice				■
White Rice Flour				■
Whole Wheat Flour				■
Wild Rice		■		
SEASONINGS				
Apple Cider Vinegar		■		
Artificial Sweeteners				■
Balsamic Vinegar			■	
Basil		■		

FOOD	ALKALIZING EFFECT		ACIDIFYING EFFECT	
	MEDIUM TO HIGH	LOW TO MEDIUM	LOW TO MEDIUM	MEDIUM TO HIGH
Bay Leaf		■		
Black Pepper		■		
Brown Sugar				■
Cardamom		■		
Cayenne Pepper				
Celery Seeds				
Cilantro				
Cinnamon				
Coriander				
Corn Syrup				■
Cumin		■		
Curry Powder			■	
Dill Seeds		■		
Dill Weed				
Fennel				
Ginger Root	■			
Greens Powder	■			
Honey			■	
Horseradish	■			
Jams and Jellies (Sweetened with Sugar)				■
Ketchup				
Mace		■		
Maple Syrup			■	
Marjoram				
Miso (Soybean Paste)	■			
Molasses		■		
Mustard (Prepared)				■
Oregano		■		
Paprika	■			

FOOD	ALKALIZING EFFECT		ACIDIFYING EFFECT	
	MEDIUM TO HIGH	LOW TO MEDIUM	LOW TO MEDIUM	MEDIUM TO HIGH
Parsley	■			
Pickle Relish				■
Red Wine Vinegar				■
Rice Syrup		■		
Rice Vinegar			■	
Sea Salt	■			
Stevia			■	
Sucanat Organic Sugar		■		
Table Salt				■
Tamari/Soy Sauce		■		
Tarragon				
Thyme				
Umeboshi Vinegar	■			
Vanilla Extract			■	
White Sugar				■
White Vinegar			■	
OILS AND BUTTERS				
Almond Butter		■		
Apple Butter		■		
Canola Oil			■	
Cashew Butter		■		
Clarified Butter		■		
Coconut Oil		■		
Cottonseed Oil				■
Flaxseed Oil		■		
Hazelnut Butter				■
Lard				■
Macadamia Nut Oil		■		
Margarine (Trans Fat-Free)		■		

FOOD	ALKALIZING EFFECT		ACIDIFYING EFFECT	
	MEDIUM TO HIGH	LOW TO MEDIUM	LOW TO MEDIUM	MEDIUM TO HIGH
Mayonnaise			■	
Olive Oil		■		
Peanut Butter				■
Peanut Oil				■
Pistachio Butter				■
Primrose Oil		■		
Safflower Oil			■	
Sesame Oil		■		
Soybean Oil				■
Sunflower Oil				■
Tahini (Sesame Butter)		■		
Vegetable Oil				■
BEVERAGES				
Alcohol				■
Apple Cider		■		
Black Tea			■	
Coffee				■
Ginger Tea	■			
Green Tea		■		
Herbal Tea		■		
Soft Drinks				■
SNACKS AND BAKING INGREDIENTS				
Baked Potato Chips		■		
Baking Powder	■			
Baking Soda	■			
Chocolate				■
Fried Foods				■
Frozen Yogurt				■
Ice Cream				■
Yeast				■

CONCLUSION

The information provided by this book will give you the tools to foster a state of optimum acid-alkaline balance for yourself and your family. By following these pH-balanced recipes on a daily basis, you will feel better, be healthier, and have more energy than you ever thought possible, all the while enjoying some of the most delicious and satisfying meals ever put on a plate. So get ready to excite your taste buds and change your life.

2. The pH-balanced Kitchen

To begin your journey towards a pH-balanced lifestyle on the right foot, you must first surround yourself with the proper tools. By "tools," I am referring not only to your kitchen appliances and equipment, but also to the ingredients that line the shelves of your pantry and refrigerator. The environment you create for yourself in the kitchen is an important step towards changing your mindset about the way you eat. A well-stocked and properly equipped kitchen will help you feel positive and capable, rather than lost and overwhelmed. By filling your cooking space with the appropriate foods and a few helpful devices, you will also be filling yourself with the confidence and ability required to follow the pH-balanced lifestyle outlined by this book. When you change your kitchen, your mindset about cooking also changes. Once your mindset has changed, the things you choose to eat will change, and that will change your life. It all begins with this first step. The following sections will move you in the right direction and let you in on a few healthful ingredients and helpful tools that all pH-balanced cooks should have in their kitchen.

A Few Words about Organic Produce

In addition to offering a number of other potential benefits to your health and the environment, organic fruits and vegetables have a positive effect on your pH level. The pesticides, herbicides, and insecticides used in conventional agriculture leave a chemical residue on food that actually raises its acidity. A fruit or vegetable that is alkalizing in its organic form may become mildly acidifying when grown with the use of synthetic additives, thereby defeating its pH-balancing purpose. This fact is especially important to remember when making recipes that feature ingredients such as potatoes, carrots, and apples, which have some of the highest rates of residual chemicals. In those cases, I strongly recommend that you buy organic, if possible. Your body will thank you.

HEALTHFUL INGREDIENTS

While the following list does not discuss *every* ingredient required to prepare the recipes in this book, it does include many of the more common pantry items needed for a majority of the meals, as well as a few of the items that might seem less familiar to you at the moment. I will also mention a few of my favorite brands of ingredients to help you choose the right products.

Breads and Wraps

Most breads and wraps are made with wheat and contain yeast, both of which encourage acid production in the body. For this reason, I would normally avoid them altogether. That being said, sprouted-grain bread made with unprocessed wheat sprouts and grains are less acidifying than the average loaf of bread and can be eaten occasionally. Keep in mind that this bread is still made with yeast, so its use should be limited. Sprouted-grain tortillas, made without yeast, are also available. Now found at most grocery stores, the Ezekiel brand of bread products offers yeast-free and wheat-free breads and tortillas.

Eggs and Egg Substitutes

Though they act as a powerful binding agent in baked goods such as muffins, cakes, and cookies, whole eggs are very acidifying. Instead, you can use egg whites, egg white products, and even the Ground Flaxseed Egg Substitute recipe found below. In the right proportion, ground flaxseed will become gelatinous in water and can take the place of eggs as a binding agent when combined with flour. For omelets and frittatas, use egg whites or a ready-made liquid-egg product, such as Simply Egg Whites or Egg Beaters.

Ground Flaxseed Egg Substitute

When you need something to bind your baked goods together without the acidity of whole eggs, try this egg substitute made with ground flaxseed. Simply mix the flaxseed with water to discover how a recipe can be both delicious and pH-balanced. In the following proportions, 1/4 cup of Ground Flaxseed Egg Substitute is equivalent to one egg.

YIELD: 2 CUPS

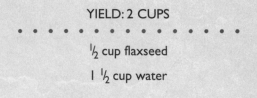

½ cup flaxseed

1 ½ cup water

1. Grind flaxseed to a fine powder in a mini food processor or electric coffee grinder.

2. Place the ground flaxseed in a small bowl and add the water. Whisk until completely combined.

3. The egg substitute can be used immediately, but it has a more egg-like consistency when allowed to sit for about 10 minutes. Keep refrigerated for up to 3 days.

Flavorings

Sumac

Traditionally found in Middle Eastern cuisine, sumac is a deep red or purple spice that is made from the ground dried fruit of the sumac plant. It is commonly used to give a tangy and lemony flavor to meat, salad, and dips such as hummus.

Liquid Smoke Flavor

Most people will agree that bacon is one of the hardest foods to cut out of your diet. It seems bacon can make anything taste, well, *better*. I can't tell you how many times I've heard friends say, "Even if I went vegetarian, I would still eat bacon. It just smells *so* good." Well, there is a way to get that smoky bacon flavor without any of the guilt or acidifying effects. It's called liquid smoke. Add a little liquid smoke to salad dressings, egg dishes, chilies, and chowders, and you won't miss the bacon at all (well, not nearly as much). I must stress, however, that the operative word in that last sentence is "little," because a little goes a long way when it comes to liquid smoke. It's always best to start with a small amount and add to taste. I recommend Woodland Natural Hickory Smoke brand flavoring, which is available in most grocery stores.

Miso

Miso is a paste made from fermented soybeans. Originating in Japan, miso is a very good source of manganese, zinc, phosphorus, and copper. It is also a good source of both protein and dietary fiber. Although miso is usually made from fermented soybeans, it can also be produced from rice, barley, or wheat. Miso comes in a variety of colors, including white, yellow, red, brown, and black. Dark-colored miso has a strong and pungent flavor, which makes it suitable for heavy foods such as beans, stews, and gravies. Light-colored miso has a delicate and subtle flavor, which makes it suitable for soups, salad dressings, and light sauces. Miso is generally sold in tightly sealed plastic or glass containers. The best selections of miso can be found in Asian markets and most health food stores.

Za'atar

Za'atar is a spice mixture that is traditionally made from sumac, sesame seeds, and herbs such as oregano, marjoram, and thyme. Sprinkled on top of meat and vegetables, or mixed with olive oil as a bread dip, Za'atar is a common feature of Middle Eastern dishes.

Flours and Grains

Amaranth Flour

This flour is made from milled amaranth seeds and contains no gluten, which makes it much less acidifying than wheat flour. It can be used in flatbreads, pastas, and certain baked goods, but must be mixed with other flours for baking yeast breads, due to its lack of gluten. Amaranth flour can be found in most health food and grocery stores.

Buckwheat Flour

Like amaranth flour, buckwheat flour has no gluten and is therefore much less acidifying than typical wheat flour. It is also very good source of protein and has a unique flavor that is especially good in both breads and pancakes. Buckwheat flour can be found in most health food and grocery stores.

Kamut Flour

Like spelt flour, kamut flour is an ancient relative of modern-day wheat. It has a buttery flavor and is easy to digest. This beautiful golden flour can be used in most recipes where you would use wheat flour. Kamut flour can be found in most health food and grocery stores.

Light Spelt Flour

An ancient relative of wheat that has been used for hundreds of years, spelt makes a less acidifying flour than whole wheat and white flour, though it is much denser. Light spelt flour is spelt flour that has had most of the bran and germ removed, making it lighter and more appropriate for use in baked goods such as cookies and cakes. Light spelt flour can be found in most health food and grocery stores.

Quinoa

Mildly alkalizing and packed with protein, iron, and potassium, quinoa refers to the edible seeds of a plant native to South America. It is extremely versatile in cooking and easily digested. If the package of quinoa does not say "prewashed," be sure to rinse and strain the seeds in a fine mesh strainer a number of times until the water runs clear, as they sometimes have a bitter coating. Quinoa can be found in most health food and grocery stores.

Rolled Oats or Instant Oatmeal

Rolled oats are mildly alkalizing and make a deliciously wholesome and chewy hot cereal that provides lasting energy all morning. This breakfast favorite is a great way to start your day and add fiber to your diet. Rolled oats or instant oatmeal can be found in most grocery stores.

Teff Flour

Made by grinding the seeds of a grass native to North Africa, teff flour can be used as a gluten-free substitute for any flour in pastas, breads, pastries, cakes, and puddings. This grain has a very high mineral content, a distinct flavor that is a bit like chocolate and hazelnut, and is only mildly acid-forming. Teff flour can be found in most health food stores.

Nutritional Supplements

Greens Powder

Most greens powders are mixtures of such nutrient-rich food as wheatgrass, barley grass, spirulina, parsley, kale, alfalfa, spirulina, spinach, chlorella, and broccoli. These greens are dried and concentrated into a powder form that can be added to smoothies and other drinks for an extra boost of vitamins and minerals. Greens powder can raise your energy level and alkalize your system. Avoid any greens powder that contains artificial colors or additives, and be sure that your greens powder does not contain yeast, probiotics, or preservatives, as they add acidity. Greens+ by Genuine Health Products is a good choice for a sweetened powder, as it is sweetened with stevia leaf and not refined sugar. Amazing Grass and Amazing Grass Green Super Food is certified organic and comes in an unsweetened variety, which you can use not only in smoothies, but also in dips and salad dressings. Greens powders are available in most health food and grocery stores.

Whey Protein Powder

Whey protein isolate is a concentrated form of protein made from milk. Whey protein powder is mildly acidifying, but when combined with alkalizing greens powder, it provides a naturally complete protein that is efficiently absorbed by the body. For people with lactose intolerance, it is best to choose whey protein products with less than 0.1g of lactose per tablespoon of powder. Make sure the brand of powder you use has no artificial ingredients. A good choice is Proteins+ by Genuine Health Products.

Oils and Fats

Canola Oil

While slightly acidifying, canola oil will do in a pinch, but try to be sure that it doesn't contain any extra additives.

Clarified Butter

Clarified butter is a spread that is produced by removing the milk solids from unsalted butter. This alkalizes the butter, while maintaining its ability to cook well at high temperatures. The preparation of clarified butter also makes it lactose-free, which is great for those who are lactose intolerant. It has no hydrogenated oil and is a popular choice for health-conscious cooks. If you can't find clarified butter at your local Indian grocery store, you can always make a batch yourself. (See the inset "Making Clarified Butter" below.) It does not require refrigeration and will keep for up to a month in an airtight container stored in a cool place.

Extra Virgin Olive

This oil is wonderful in salad dressings and has a slightly alkalizing affect on dishes, but its distinct flavor does not always suit baked goods. When baking, use clarified butter or a light-tasting olive

---

Making Clarified Butter

If there are no Indian or Middle Eastern markets nearby, it may be difficult for you to find prepackaged clarified butter for purchase. Thankfully, it can be easily made at home and stored for future use.

YIELD: 4 CUPS

1. Place 2 pounds of unsalted butter in a 2 ½-quart saucepan over medium-high heat. Do not stir the butter while it is cooking. The butter will come to a boil and sputter slightly as the water cooks out of it.

2. Once it comes to a boil, reduce the heat to medium. Foam will appear on the top. This first foam will cook off. Clarified butter is done once the butter has turned transparent and golden under the second layer of foam. You should also see the sediment at the bottom of the pan start

to turn golden brown. You can check the color of the sediment by gently tilting the pan. The entire process should take approximately 20 minutes. Clarified butter will burn quickly, so check often. When done, immediately remove from heat.

3. Let cool slightly and gently pour into heatproof containers through a fine mesh strainer or any strainer lined with doubled cheesecloth. Discard the sediment. While perfectly clarified butter does not need to be refrigerated, I would still recommend storing it in a tightly sealed glass jar in the fridge, in case a few milk solids happen to remain.

oil instead. Olive oil has a low smoking point, which means that it burns and breaks down at a lower temperature than do other types of oil. When cooking with olive oil, use it only to lightly sauté foods, not fry them.

Olive Oil-based and Canola Oil-based Cooking Spray

When using cooking sprays, a light misting usually works, especially if you are also using parchment paper. Olive oil-based spray is best for lightly roasting vegetables and canola-based spray is best for baked goods, where you would not want the olive oil flavor.

Sweeteners

Brown Rice Syrup

Brown rice syrup is a nutritious sweetener that is about one half as sweet as sugar. It is less acidifying than other sweeteners and makes a good substitute in place of sugar, honey, corn syrup, and maple syrup. Use 1 $1/4$ cup rice syrup for one cup of sugar, making sure you use $1/4$ cup less of another liquid in the recipe to compensate. Lundberg Family Farms Brown Rice Syrup is a high-quality example of this sweetener and can be found in most grocery and health food stores.

Molasses

Molasses is an alkalizing sweetener that is made from either mature sugar cane or sugar beets. Unlike refined sugar, molasses contains significant amounts of vitamins and minerals. Blackstrap molasses is a good source of calcium, magnesium, potassium, and iron.

Stevia

Made from the leaves of the stevia plant, stevia contains several natural chemicals called glycosides, which taste sugary, but do not provide calories. Stevia leaf extract is intensely sweet with a mild licorice aftertaste. Although it is used in only one of the recipes in this book, you can substitute stevia for sugar wherever you wish, keeping in mind the aftertaste and the fact that it does not add the volume to recipes that Sucanat, rice syrup, and molasses provide. Stevia can be found in most grocery and health food stores.

Sucanat

Unlike most brown and white sugars, Sucanat is unprocessed and unrefined. It is made from freshly extracted sugar cane juice, which is reduced until a rich, dark syrup forms. This syrup is then dried to create dry, porous granules. This simple process gives it a nice molasses-style flavor and also makes it a significantly less acidifying sweetener than regular sugar.

Other Ingredients

Almond Milk

Almond milk is a milky liquid made from ground almonds, which are alkalizing, and purified water. It contains no cholesterol or lactose and is a better substitute for acidifying animal milk than soy milk, which also has acidic properties. Commercially made almond milk products come in plain, vanilla, and chocolate flavors, and are often enriched with vitamins. I use unsweetened almond milk to avoid the acidity that sugar can bring. Blue Diamond Original Unsweetened and Vanilla Flavor Unsweetened are my preferred brands. You will find them used in many of the recipes throughout this cookbook. Almond milk is available in most grocery stores.

Cheese Curds

While cheeses in general are acidifying, cheese curds provide us with a less acidic choice for our recipes. Curds are made before the cheese is processed into blocks and aged. They have a mild cheddar flavor and can be made from cow's milk and goat's milk. Thankfully, they also melt well in the microwave and can be spread easily. Cheese curds are usually sold in the deli section of your local grocery store. If your local grocer does not carry cheese curds, you can always use mozzarella or provolone instead.

Dried Goji Berries

Goji berries, also called wolfberries, are a highly alkalizing fruit. These little berries have a mild, tangy taste that is both sweet and sour. They have a similar texture to raisins and are known for their excellent nutritional value and antioxidant content. Thanks to their rise in popularity, goji berries can be found in most health food and grocery stores.

Mayonnaise

When selecting a mayonnaise, try to find one that has been made without sugar, eggs, and soy oil, as these ingredients are acidifying. Favor brands made with canola or olive oil and flavored with apple cider vinegar, which can help keep the condiment relatively alkaline. Finally, while many of these types of mayonnaise list "soy protein isolate" on their ingredient labels, do your best to choose one that features it at the *end* of the list, as too much soy can increase your level of acidity. Brands that fit these criteria include Earth

Island Original Vegenaise, Organic Eggless Light Mayo by Spectrum Naturals, and Eggless Mayonnaise-Style Dressing by Canoline. Most health food markets—and a growing number of regular grocery stores—carry these brands.

Wakame

A highly alkalizing type of dried seaweed, Wakame must be soaked in water or cooked in broth before being used. It is often used in Asian soups, salads, and even seasoned and eaten on its own. Wakame expands considerably, so remember that small amounts go a long way. It can be found in most health food and Asian markets.

Water

Water, in its purest form, is neutral. That means it has no effect on your pH balance. On the other hand, tap water is usually slightly acidic, depending on its source and whether or not it has been chlorinated. Thankfully, the concentration of acids in drinking water is relatively small and does not affect your body's pH in any significant way. In general, tap water's effect on your pH has more to do with the elements it lacks than the acids it contains.

Minerals such as calcium and magnesium, as well as compounds such as bicarbonate, are highly alkalizing. They are most abundantly available in bottled mineral water, which is obtained from mineral springs or other water sources that contain dissolved solids. They are not, however, typically found in beneficial amounts in most sources of tap water.

One last thing to consider is the form of these minerals. The best type of water for your pH level is that which has the lowest amount of chloride, as nonchloride forms of calcium and magnesium are alkalizing, while their chloride varieties are acidifying. You can contact your local water board to find out detailed information about the mineral content of your tap water.

I suggest that you become more pH-balanced by increasing your intake of alkalizing foods, first and foremost, rather than worrying too much about your water. But if you are fighting a particularly bad case of acidosis, adding mineral water to your diet or filtering your tap water through a water ionizer (see the inset "Ionized Water" on page 75) may help.

HELPFUL KITCHEN EQUIPMENT

Once you've stocked your pantry and refrigerator with all the necessary ingredients, you should then surround yourself with the some helpful kitchen equipment. The right appliances and cookware will make following the recipes seem easy and save you time and energy. By keeping just a few standard items within arm's reach, your cooking experience will become a pleasure and a breeze.

Blender

A blender is a great appliance for blending soups, sauces, dips, and salad dressings. In addition to a full-sized blender, a stick, or immersion, blender gives you the convenience of blending items directly in your cooking pot. Its small size also allows for convenient storage.

Cast-Iron Skillet

Cast iron is very heavy and heats evenly. It is great for making tortillas and other flat breads, as well as toasting nuts and seeds. If you do not have a cast-iron skillet, a non-stick frying pan will still allow you to cook without the need for a lot of acidifying oil and butter.

Food Mill

Also called a moulinette, this tool is used for mashing and straining soft foods. With the help of a metal blade turned by a crank, the food is crushed through a perforated plate, which strains the mashed item into a bowl below. Often used to mash potatoes and remove seeds from fruit, this device is something between a colander and an electric blender.

Food Processor with Grating Attachment

Food processors can do everything, from roughly chopping ingredients to puréeing them with ease. A grating attachment makes quick work of tougher items, such as potatoes, cabbage, and cheese.

Mandoline

A mandoline comes in handy when you need to slice vegetables and fruit extremely thinly. It is made up of an adjustable surface and a fixed surface that has been fitted with a blade. The food is slid along the adjustable surface until it reaches the blade, which cuts it according to the set width. It is also able to julienne ingredients such as carrots, potatoes, and zucchini in a snap.

Parchment Paper

Nothing sticks to this wonderful paper! When you line your baking pan with parchment paper, your baked goods simply slide right off—and the pan stays clean!

Potato Ricer

This device looks like a large garlic press and has a similar function to the food mill. It basically forces soft foods through rice-sized holes, squeezing out any excess water in the process. Like the food mill, it is often used to make mashed potatoes.

Silicone Muffin, Loaf, and Cake Pans

Silicone pans allow baked goods to pop easily out of their mold without the use of acidifying butter or oil. They are also a better choice when baking with non-wheat flour, which is less acidifying than regular flour, but usually more fragile due to the lack of gluten.

Whisk

This tool is very handy for blending flours and other dry ingredients together when preparing a batter. I also use a whisk for blending thickeners into sauces and emulsifying oil when preparing salad dressings.

Lemon Zester

When a recipe calls for a lot of lemon zest, a lemon zester makes the job so much easier. And of course, it works for any other fruit as well! Opt for a microplane version, which does a much better job than most other models. When zesting, be careful to remove only the outer rind of the fruit and not the white pith, as it would add bitterness to the recipe.

CONCLUSION

We humans tend to be creatures of habit, clinging to the familiar. We are often uneasy about stepping outside of our comfort zone, even when both instinct and intellect tell us it may be in our best interest to do so. Our wonderful and devious minds are masters at inventing endless reasons for not taking a new path.

I designed this chapter to encourage you to take that first step towards better health. If you are reading this then you are already on your way. While some of the tools may seem unfamiliar and some of the ingredients may sound curious, as you work your way through this book, that sense of strangeness will quickly disappear. Many of your favorite meals are here, just with a few adjustments. And the dishes that are new to you are so good, they are sure to end up on your list of old stand-bys.

The basis for real change is your attitude. The most important thing is that you approach pH-balanced living in a positive way, embracing it in the spirit of delight and anticipating the good health it can bring to your life. If you can manage that, the rest is easy—with the help of the right recipes, of course.

PART TWO

Recipes for Good Health

3. Breakfast

Getting a quick and nutritious breakfast is not always an easy task. When we're not grabbing a donut or muffin on the way to work, we're pouring a bowl of sugary cereal at home before leaving. By following this habit day after day, you not only deprive your body of healthy nutrients, but also cause it to have a highly acidic pH level. The truth is, you can have a great morning meal without being late for work—and it can be pH-balanced. All you have to do is replace some typical recipe ingredients with less-acidifying substitutes.

The recipes in this chapter are designed to help you enjoy delicious breakfast dishes that are as quick to prepare as they are wholesome and pH-balanced. Breakfast can be as simple as almond butter and banana slices on toasted sprouted-grain bread, or even just a handful of alkalizing fresh fruit and nuts. If you have the time to arrange a few things in advance, you can enjoy delicious pancakes or hash browns. In the colder months, you can even make a large pot of oatmeal and reheat portions throughout the week. Add some alkalizing berries and you are good to go.

No matter what your favorite morning treat might be, the following recipes will help you keep eating the meals that you enjoy, while avoiding the acidity that they normally create.

CINNAMON RAISIN BREAD

Delicious, satisfying, and made without any acidifying yeast, dairy, or processed sugar, this bread is well worth the time it takes to bake. You will thank yourself for throwing a couple of slices in the toaster and topping it off with your favorite pH-balanced spread.

YIELD: ONE 9-X-5-INCH LOAF

• • • • • • •

4 cups light spelt flour

1 1/2 cups dark raisins

1/4 cup raw sesame seeds

1/4 cup Sucanat sugar

1 tablespoon ground cinnamon

2 teaspoons baking powder

1 teaspoon baking soda

1/4 teaspoon sea salt

2 1/8 cups unsweetened almond milk

1. Preheat the oven to 350°F. Lightly coat a 9-x-5-inch loaf pan with vegetable oil, clarified butter, or cooking spray, or line the bottom of the pan with parchment paper, and set aside.

2. In a large bowl, whisk together the flour, raisins, sesame seeds, sugar, cinnamon, baking powder, baking soda, and salt. Make a well in the center of the dry ingredients.

3. Add the milk to the dry ingredients and mix thoroughly with a spoon until a stiff batter forms.

4. Spread the batter evenly in the prepared loaf pan. Gently knock the bottom of the pan on your kitchen counter to remove any air pockets in the batter.

5. Cover the pan with aluminum foil to keep the top of the loaf from splitting. Bake for 40 minutes.

6. Remove the pan from oven, discard the foil, and return the pan to the oven. Bake for 30 additional minutes, or until a toothpick inserted in the center of the loaf comes out clean. Let cool.

7. Toast slices and serve them along with a non-hydrogenated margarine or Clarified Butter (page 19).

> **"The best and safest thing is to keep a balance in your life, acknowledge the great powers around us and in us. If you can do that, and live that way, you are really a wise man."**
>
> **– Euripides, playwright**

BUCKWHEAT PANCAKES

*These pancakes are light and fluffy, and sure to become a family favorite
for breakfast and brunch. All that, and no eggs or wheat flour
to acidify your stomach!*

1. Preheat the oven to 200°F.

2. In a large bowl, whisk together the flours, rice bran, sugar, baking powder, and salt. Make a well in the center of the dry ingredients.

3. Add the milk to the dry ingredients and mix quickly with a spoon just until combined. Set aside.

4. Lightly coat a 10-inch skillet with vegetable oil, clarified butter, or cooking spray. Heat the skillet over medium-high heat until a drop of water sizzles when it hits the surface.

5. Pour $^1/_4$ cup of the pancake batter on the skillet and cook until bubbles form on top of the pancake and its edges are no longer shiny. Flip the pancake over and continue cooking for about 1 minute, or until the second side is golden brown. Repeat with the remaining batter until you have 6 pancakes.

6. As the pancakes are done, transfer them to an oven-safe dish and keep them warm in the preheated oven. Serve the pancakes with Berry Sauce (page 100), molasses, or rice syrup for a pH-balanced treat.

YIELD: 3 SERVINGS
(2 PANCAKES EACH)
• • • • • • •

$^3/_4$ cup light spelt flour

$^1/_4$ cup buckwheat flour

1 tablespoon rice bran

1 tablespoon Sucanat sugar

2 teaspoons baking powder

$^1/_4$ teaspoon sea salt

1 cup unsweetened
almond milk

HELPFUL TIP

To have a large batch of pancake batter ready to go at a moment's notice, double or triple the dry ingredients in the recipe. Store the dry batter in a glass container with a tight-fitting lid in a cool, dry place. When it's time to prepare the pancakes, simply add $1^1/_2$ cups of unsweetened almond milk to every 2 cups of dry batter.

APPLE JACK PANCAKES

With a taste that will remind you of a delectable apple Danish, Apple Jack Pancakes are sure to become one of your favorite morning treats. By sweetening it with Sucanat sugar and using the natural sweetness of the apples, you can enjoy this delicious meal free of the acidity normally found in similar store-bought breakfasts.

YIELD: 4 SERVINGS (2 PANCAKES EACH)
• • • • • • •

I cup finely chopped dried apple slices

$3/4$ cup boiling water

$3/4$ cup light spelt flour

$1/4$ cup oat flour

2 tablespoons Sucanat sugar

I tablespoon baking powder

I tablespoon rice bran

2 teaspoons ground cinnamon

$1/4$ teaspoon sea salt

$3/4$ cup unsweetened almond milk

1. Preheat the oven to 200°F.

2. In a small heatproof bowl, pour the boiling water over the apples and set aside for 10 minutes.

3. In a large bowl, whisk together the flours, sugar, baking powder, rice bran, cinnamon, and salt. Make a well in the center of the dry ingredients.

4. Add the milk to the dry ingredients and mix quickly with a spoon just until combined.

5. Gently fold the apples and water into the dry ingredients until well combined.

6. Coat a 10-inch skillet with vegetable oil, clarified butter, or cooking spray. Heat the skillet over medium-high heat until a drop of water sizzles when it hits the surface.

7. Pour $1/4$ cup of the pancake batter on the skillet and cook until bubbles form on top of the pancake and its edges are no longer shiny. Flip the pancake over and continue cooking for about 1 minute, or until the second side is golden brown. Repeat with the remaining batter until you have 8 pancakes.

6. As the pancakes are done, transfer them to an oven-safe dish and keep them warm in the preheated oven while you cook the remaining batter. Serve with Apple Butter Sauce (page 96).

PUMPKIN PIE PANCAKES

These spicy pancakes are perfect for a weekend breakfast or brunch. Serve them with sliced fresh fruit such as oranges, peaches, and straw- berries for a truly memorable and pH-balanced morning experience.

1. Preheat the oven to 200°F.

2. In a medium-sized bowl, combine the pumpkin purée, sugar, water, butter, pumpkin pie spice, orange zest, ginger, and salt. Mix well with a spoon until blended and set aside.

3. In a large bowl, whisk together the flours and baking powder. Make a well in the center of the dry ingredients.

4. Add the pumpkin mixture and milk to the dry ingredients and mix well with a spoon just until combined.

5. Coat a 10-inch skillet with vegetable oil, clarified butter, or cooking spray. Heat the skillet over medium-high heat until a drop of water siz- zles when it hits the surface.

6. Pour $^1/_4$ cup of the pancake batter on the skillet and cook until bub- bles form on top of the pancake and its edges are no longer shiny. Flip the pancake over and continue cooking for about 1 minute, or until the second side is golden brown. Repeat with the remaining batter until you have 8 pancakes.

7. As the pancakes are done, transfer them to an oven-safe dish and keep them warm in the preheated oven while you cook the remaining batter. Serve with brown rice syrup and fresh fruit. Use the remaining canned pumpkin to make Pumpkin Ginger Pear Soup (page 69).

YIELD: 4 SERVINGS (2 PANCAKES EACH)

• • • • • • •

$^1/_2$ cup canned unsweetened pumpkin purée

$^1/_4$ cup Sucanat sugar

$^1/_4$ cup water

1 tablespoon melted clarified butter

$^1/_2$ teaspoon pumpkin pie spice

1 tablespoon orange zest

2 teaspoons grated ginger root

$^1/_4$ teaspoon sea salt

$^1/_2$ cup kamut flour

$^1/_2$ cup light spelt flour

1 tablespoon baking powder

$^3/_4$ cup unsweetened almond milk

"Harmony makes small things grow, lack of it makes great things decay."

— Sallust, historian

BREAKFAST HASH

The mixture of potatoes, onion, bell pepper, celery, and carrot makes this dish a hearty breakfast. It is also a great way to use up leftover fish, ground beef, and poultry. When buying the hash brown potatoes, be sure to choose a brand with no added fat or preservatives, which would raise the pH of the recipe.

YIELD: 4 SERVINGS

1 tablespoon light olive oil

3 cups frozen hash brown potatoes

1 medium-sized onion, finely chopped

$\frac{1}{2}$ cup finely chopped red or green bell pepper

$\frac{1}{2}$ cup finely chopped celery

$\frac{1}{2}$ cup grated carrot

$\frac{1}{2}$ to $\frac{3}{4}$ cup cooked flaked fish, ground beef, or chopped poultry

$\frac{1}{2}$ teaspoon dried summer savory

Sea salt to taste

1. In a 12-inch skillet, heat the oil over medium-low heat. Add the potatoes and cook, stirring occasionally, for 5 to 7 minutes, or until heated through. Transfer them to a large bowl and set aside.

2. Add the onion, pepper, celery, and carrot to the skillet and sauté, stirring occasionally, just until tender.

3. Add the meat to the vegetables and stir until heated throughout.

4. Return the potatoes to the skillet. Add the summer savory and salt. Cook the potatoes, stirring occasionally, until fully reheated. Serve with a small amount of organic ketchup.

SWEET POTATO LATKES

Sweet potatoes are a very alkalizing food. This recipe requires a bit of time to prepare, but the result is completely worth it. Also called potato pancakes, latkes are as good cold as they are straight off the skillet.

YIELD: 15 LATKES

$\frac{3}{8}$ cup light spelt flour

1 teaspoon baking powder

1 teaspoon sea salt

Freshly ground black pepper to taste

3 cups coarsely grated unpeeled sweet potato (about 1 pound)

1 large onion, grated

$\frac{3}{8}$ cup egg substitute

1 teaspoon clarified butter

1. Preheat the oven to 200°F.

2. In a large bowl, whisk together the flour, baking powder, salt, and pepper.

3. Add the sweet potato and onion to the bowl and mix thoroughly with a spoon. Add the egg substitute and stir until well blended.

4. In a 10-inch nonstick skillet, heat the butter over medium-low heat.

5. Pour $\frac{1}{4}$ cup of the potato mixture on the skillet, lightly pressing down the center of the mixture and gathering its edges together to make a round and flattened latke. Repeat this process until your skillet is covered with latkes. Cook the latkes for 5 to 7 minutes per side, or until browned and slightly caramelized on each side.

6. Serve the latkes with unsweetened applesauce or sliced fresh fruit such as melons, oranges, or strawberries.

POTATO FRITTATA

This filling breakfast frittata also makes a delicious light lunch when served with a tossed green salad. As mentioned in the recipe for Breakfast Hash, you should always choose a brand of hash brown potatoes with no added fat or preservatives so that your meal remains pH-balanced.

1. Preheat the oven broiler to 400°F.

2. In a 10-inch oven-safe skillet, the heat the oil over medium-low heat. Add the potatoes and cook, stirring occasionally, for 5 to 7 minutes, or until heated through and slightly crispy. Transfer the potatoes to a large bowl and set aside.

3. Add the onion, pepper, and zucchini to the skillet and sauté for 5 minutes, or just until tender. Return the potatoes to the skillet and spread the mixture evenly over the bottom. Reduce the heat to low.

4. In a small bowl, combine the egg substitute, milk, cheese, basil, garlic, and salt. Mix well with a spoon and pour over the potato-vegetable mixture. Cook, without stirring, for 3 minutes, or until the egg substitute is almost set. Remove from the heat, cover, and let sit for 3 minutes.

5. Uncover the frittata and place it under the preheated broiler for 3 minutes, or until brown. Cut into wedges and serve immediately.

YIELD: 8 SERVINGS
• • • • • • • •

$1\frac{1}{2}$ tablespoons light olive oil

2 cups frozen hash brown potatoes

1 small onion, finely chopped

$\frac{1}{4}$ cup finely chopped red or green bell pepper

$\frac{1}{2}$ cup grated zucchini

1 cup egg substitute

$\frac{1}{8}$ cup unsweetened almond milk

1 tablespoon grated Parmesan or crumbled feta cheese

$\frac{1}{2}$ teaspoon dried basil

$\frac{1}{2}$ teaspoon garlic powder

$\frac{1}{2}$ teaspoon sea salt

Who Discovered pH?

The idea that the acidity of a substance could be determined by the number of hydrogen ions it releases when dissolved was first proposed by Swedish scientist Svante Arrhenius at the end of the nineteenth century. He suggested that the higher the concentration of hydrogen ions in a substance, the more acidic that substance would be. In the years that followed, a number of scientists refined that idea, with the Brønsted-Lowry definition declaring that both acids and bases (also known as alkalies) have an effect on the number of hydrogen ions released by a substance. According to this theory, acids release hydrogen ions, while bases accept them. Finally, in 1909, Danish chemist Sören Sörensen created the pH scale (referring to the potential, or power, of hydrogen ions) to measure acidity and alkalinity, with 0 being highly acidic, 7 being neutral, and 14 being highly alkaline.

BREAKFAST BURRITOS

This awesome breakfast is bound to transport you south of border with your first bite. And the more vegetables you use to make your burritos, the more alkaline it will be. So go for it!

1. In a $2^1/_2$-quart saucepan, heat the oil over medium-low heat. Add the onion, peppers, and zucchini. Sauté for 5 minutes, or until the onion is transparent.

2. Add the cilantro and salt to the vegetables and stir until well blended.

4. Add the egg substitute to the vegetables and stir until the eggs are set.

5. Arrange the wraps on a flat surface. Spread equal amounts of the egg mixture down the middle of each wrap. Top each burrito with an equally divided portion of the cheese and 1 tablespoon of salsa.

6. Roll up each burrito and serve warm with additional salsa on the side.

YIELD: 4 BURRITOS

• • • • • • • • • •

I tablespoon olive oil

I medium-sized onion, finely chopped

I medium-sized red bell pepper, coarsely chopped

I medium-sized green bell pepper, coarsely chopped

I small zucchini, finely chopped

$^1/_4$ cup finely chopped fresh cilantro

$^1/_2$ teaspoon sea salt

I cup egg substitute

$^1/_4$ cup finely chopped curd cheese or mozzarella cheese

4 tablespoons organic salsa

4 sprouted-grain wraps or Multigrain Tortillas (page 47)

SMOKED SALMON BISCUITS

Who can resist warm biscuits first thing in the morning? Here is a more alkaline (and more delicious) substitute for your everyday smoked salmon on a bagel.

1. Preheat the oven to 425°F. Lightly coat a 9-x-13-inch baking sheet with vegetable oil, clarified butter, or cooking spray, and set aside.

2. In a small bowl, toss together the scallions, smoked salmon, dill, and 1 tablespoon of flour.

3. In a large bowl, whisk together the remaining 2 cups of flour, baking powder, and salt.

YIELD: 9 BISCUITS

• • • • • • • • • •

2 finely chopped scallions

2 tablespoons finely diced smoked salmon (about I ounce)

$^1/_4$ teaspoon dill seed, or I teaspoon finely chopped fresh dill

2 cups plus I tablespoon light spelt flour, divided

$1^1/_2$ tablespoons baking powder

$^1/_4$ teaspoon sea salt

3 tablespoons melted clarified butter

I cup less 2 tablespoons water, brought to room temperature

4. Gently fold the salmon mixture into the flour mixture until evenly distributed.

5. In a small bowl, combine the butter and water. Mix well with a spoon and pour into the salmon mixture. Stir together in 10 to 12 strokes, or until the batter is well combined.

6. Spoon out the batter on the prepared baking sheet in 9 mounds of equal size, leaving room for the mounds to expand. Be sure to make the mounds high rather than wide, as they will spread while baking.

7. Bake the biscuits for 10 to 12 minutes, or until they are firm to the touch and lightly browned on the bottom. Let them cool slightly. Split each biscuit and serve with light cream cheese or non-hydrogenated margarine.

HOMEMADE GRANOLA

Granola has been a family staple for years. It is tasty, hearty, and very easy to make at home. When prepared with alkaline ingredients, as it is in the following recipe, it's also good for you.

1. Preheat the oven to 325°F.

2. In an oven-safe measuring cup, combine the butter, rice syrup, and sugar. Mix well with a spoon until blended.

3. In a 9-x-13-inch baking dish with high sides, whisk together the oats, coconut, pumpkin seeds, sunflower seeds, almonds, flour, sesame seeds, ground cinnamon, and salt.

4. Add the syrup mixture to the oat mixture and toss well.

5. Spread the granola evenly in the baking dish and bake, stirring every 10 minutes, for 30 minutes, or until dry and browning.

6. Add the raisins and apple slices to the granola and stir until well blended. Store in an airtight container and use within two weeks. Freeze for longer storage.

YIELD: 10 CUPS

. . . .

$\frac{1}{4}$ cup clarified butter

$\frac{1}{4}$ cup rice syrup

$\frac{1}{4}$ cup Sucanat sugar

4 cups old-fashioned rolled oats

$\frac{3}{4}$ cup unsweetened shredded coconut

$\frac{3}{4}$ cup shelled raw pumpkin seeds

$\frac{3}{4}$ cup shelled raw sunflower seeds

$\frac{1}{2}$ cup coarsely chopped raw almonds

$\frac{1}{4}$ cup coconut flour (optional)

$\frac{1}{4}$ cup raw sesame seeds

1 to 2 teaspoons ground cinnamon

$\frac{1}{2}$ teaspoon sea salt

$1\frac{1}{2}$ cups dark raisins

1 cup finely chopped dried apple slices

ALMOND OATMEAL WITH RAISINS AND CINNAMON

The almonds in this recipe help to alkalize your breakfast, while also adding a toasty flavor, some healthy protein, and a little crunch. To save time in the morning, make a large pot of this oatmeal at the start of the week, refrigerate it, and reheat portions as desired.

1. In a $2^1/_2$-quart saucepan, heat the butter over low heat. Add the almonds and toast until golden brown.

2. Add the water, oats, raisins, sugar, cinnamon, and salt to the saucepan and bring to a boil over high heat.

3. Reduce the heat to medium-low and simmer, stirring constantly, for 10 to 12 minutes, or until the oatmeal reaches desired consistency.

4. Portion the oatmeal into individual bowls, sprinkle with flaxseed, top with a little milk and serve hot.

YIELD: 10 SERVINGS

2 teaspoons clarified butter

$1/_4$ cup slivered almonds

4 cups water

2 cups old-fashioned rolled oats

1 cup dark raisins

2 tablespoons Sucanat sugar

1 teaspoon ground cinnamon

$1/_4$ teaspoon sea salt

Ground golden flaxseed

Unsweetened almond milk

PUMPKIN SEED OATMEAL WITH GOJI BERRIES

Tasting like an orange-cranberry muffin, this oatmeal gives you a very different flavor than your everyday variety, and without all the calories. While they are simply delicious, the pumpkin seeds and goji berries also boost the alkaline value of this yummy breakfast.

1. In a $1^1/_2$-quart saucepan, heat the butter over low heat. Add the pumpkin seeds and toast until golden brown.

2. Add the water, goji berries, and orange zest to the saucepan and bring to a boil over high heat.

3. Add the oats, sugar, nutmeg, and salt to the saucepan and bring back to a boil over high heat.

4. Reduce the heat to medium-low and simmer, stirring constantly, for 10 to 12 minutes, or until the oatmeal reaches desired consistency.

5. Portion the oatmeal into individual bowls, sprinkle with flaxseed, top with a little milk, and serve hot.

YIELD: 10 SERVINGS

2 teaspoons clarified butter

$1/_4$ cup shelled raw pumpkin seeds

4 cups water

$1/_2$ cup dried goji berries

Zest of 1 orange

2 cups old-fashioned rolled oats

2 tablespoons Sucanat sugar

$1/_2$ teaspoon ground nutmeg

$1/_4$ teaspoon sea salt

Ground golden flaxseed

Unsweetened almond milk

4. Beverages

Chilled shakes and smoothies are always a refreshing treat, especially during the hot summer months. Almost any combination of fruit, whey protein isolate powder, and ground flaxseed will make a healthy and delicious beverage. Throw a little alkalizing greens powder into the mix and you've got an energy-boosting drink that is sure to keep your system running smoothly. Adding vegetables to your shakes and smoothies will increase their nutritional value even more. Experiment by including a little baby spinach, kale, or even romaine lettuce in these cool concoctions. You'll get all the health benefits of vegetables, while the fruit will make the whole thing taste sweet and yummy. The following recipes are a few of my favorite combinations.

BANANA WHEY SHAKE

*A tasty and smooth way to start your day,
this shake packs a nutritional punch that will
keep you going with energy to spare.*

1. In a blender, combine the banana and water. Purée until smooth.

2. Add the milk, whey powder, greens powder, flaxseed, cinnamon, and nutmeg to the blender and process until well blended.

3. Add the ice cubes to the blender and process until smooth and creamy.

4. Pour into two tall glasses and enjoy.

YIELD: 2 SERVINGS
· · · · · · · · ·

1 medium-sized banana, cut into chunks

$^1/_2$ cup water

1 cup unsweetened almond milk

2 scoops vanilla-flavored whey protein isolate powder sweetened with stevia

1 tablespoon unflavored greens powder

1 tablespoon ground flaxseed

Pinch ground cinnamon

Pinch ground nutmeg

$^1/_2$ cup ice cubes

BLENDER BERRIES SHAKE

*In addition to alkalizing this shake, the greens powder and
berries tend to give it a grey hue. Just close your eyes and drink.
You do not want to miss out on this tasty beverage.*

1. In a blender, combine the berries and water. Purée until smooth.

2. Add the milk, whey powder, greens powder, and flaxseed to the blender and process until well blended.

3. Add the ice cubes to the blender and process until smooth and creamy.

4. Pour into two tall glasses and enjoy.

YIELD: 2 SERVINGS
· · · · · · · · ·

1 cup unsweetened mixed frozen berries

$^1/_2$ cup water

1 cup unsweetened almond milk

2 scoops vanilla-flavored whey protein isolate powder sweetened with stevia

1 tablespoon unflavored greens powder

1 tablespoon ground flaxseed

$^1/_2$ cup ice cubes

Piña Colada Smoothie

*This is not an everyday smoothie, but rather a treat
for special occasions. The taste will have you
seeing palm trees in no time.*

1. In a blender, combine the pineapple and water. Purée until
smooth.

2. Add the coconut milk, almond milk, whey powder, and flaxseed
to the blender and process until well blended.

3. Add the ice cubes to the blender and process until smooth and
creamy.

4. Pour into two tall glasses and enjoy.

YIELD: 2 SERVINGS

½ cup fresh or canned
pineapple tidbits

½ cup water

1 cup unsweetened
coconut milk

1 cup unsweetened
almond milk

2 scoops vanilla-flavored whey
protein isolate powder
sweetened with stevia

1 tablespoon ground flaxseed

1 cup ice cubes

Grapefruit Grasshopper Shake

*If you like grapefruit, you will love this shake.
The tartness of the juice is softened by the
vanilla-flavored whey powder.*

1. In a blender, combine all of the ingredients except for the ice
cubes. Purée until smooth.

2. Add the ice cubes to the blender and process until smooth and
creamy.

3. Pour into two tall glasses and enjoy.

YIELD: 2 SERVINGS

1 cup unsweetened
grapefruit juice

1 cup unsweetened
almond milk

2 scoops vanilla-flavored whey
protein isolate powder
sweetened with stevia

1 tablespoon unflavored
greens powder

1 tablespoon ground flaxseed

1 cup ice cubes

CARROT PINEAPPLE SMOOTHIE

This smoothie is a great way to get your vegetables without even knowing it. The pineapple juice complements the carrot perfectly.

1. In a blender, combine the carrot and water. Purée until smooth.

2. Add the pineapple juice, whey powder, and flaxseed to the blender and process until well blended.

3. Add the ice cubes to the blender and process until smooth and creamy.

4. Pour into two tall glasses and enjoy.

YIELD: 2 SERVINGS

● ● ● ● ● ● ● ●

1 medium-sized carrot, peeled and coarsely chopped

1 cup water

2 cups unsweetened pineapple juice

2 scoops vanilla-flavored whey protein isolate powder sweetened with stevia

1 tablespoon ground flaxseed

$\frac{1}{2}$ cup ice cubes

APPLE PIE IN A GLASS

Not quite an apple pie in a glass but so much better for you and quick to go!

1. In a blender, combine the apples and apple juice. Purée until smooth.

2. Add the milk, whey powder, flaxseed, sugar, and cinnamon to the blender and process until well blended.

3. Add the ice cubes to the blender and process until smooth and creamy.

4. Pour into two tall glasses and enjoy.

YIELD: 2 SERVINGS

● ● ● ● ● ● ● ●

2 medium-sized apples, cored, peeled, and coarsely chopped

1 cup unsweetened apple juice

1 $\frac{1}{2}$ cup unsweetened vanilla-flavored almond milk

2 scoops vanilla-flavored whey protein isolate powder sweetened with stevia

1 tablespoon ground flaxseed

1 teaspoon Sucanat sugar

$\frac{1}{2}$ teaspoon ground cinnamon

$\frac{1}{2}$ cup ice cubes

MANGO FUSION

This drink has tropical flair that is sure to open your eyes first thing in the morning.

1. In a blender, combine the mango, pineapple juice, and banana. Purée until smooth.

2. Add the milk and flaxseed to the blender and process until well blended.

3. Add the ice cubes to the blender and process until smooth and creamy.

4. Pour into two tall glasses and enjoy.

YIELD: 2 SERVINGS

I cup fresh or frozen mango pieces

I cup unsweetened pineapple juice

½ medium-sized banana, cut into chunks

½ cup unsweetened almond milk

I tablespoon ground flaxseed

½ cup ice cubes

ALMOND BUTTER CHOCOLATE SHAKE

You just knew there had to be a chocolate shake included in this chapter, right? Kids and adults alike love chocolate. So here is a chocolate shake that won't make you feel guilty.

1. In a blender, combine all of the ingredients except for the ice cubes. Purée until smooth.

2. Add the ice cubes to the blender and process until smooth and creamy.

3. Pour into two tall glasses and enjoy.

YIELD: 2 SERVINGS

2½ cups unsweetened almond milk

2 scoops vanilla-flavored whey protein isolate powder sweetened with stevia

2 tablespoons almond butter

2 tablespoons cocoa powder

I tablespoon Sucanat sugar

½ cup ice cubes

YIELD: 2 SERVINGS
• • • • • • • •
I cup fresh or frozen
strawberries

I cup water

I cup unsweetened vanilla-
flavored almond milk

2 scoops vanilla-flavored whey
protein isolate powder
sweetened with stevia

I tablespoon ground flaxseed

$\frac{1}{2}$ cup ice cubes

STRAWBERRY VANILLA DELIGHT

You just can't beat the combination of strawberry and vanilla.
This smoothie is refreshing and so delicious on a summer day.

1. In a blender, combine the strawberries and water. Purée until smooth.

2. Add the milk, whey powder, and flaxseed to the blender and process until well blended.

3. Add the ice cubes and process until smooth and creamy.

4. Pour into two tall glasses and enjoy.

YIELD: 2 SERVINGS
• • • • • • • •
I cup unsweetened canned
mandarin orange slices, drained

I cup orange juice

2 tablespoons fresh lemon juice

I cup unsweetened
almond milk

2 scoops vanilla-flavored
whey protein isolate powder
sweetened with stevia

I tablespoons Sucanat sugar

$\frac{1}{2}$ cup ice cubes

ORANGE YA HAPPY!

This smoothie makes me happy, as it has lots of vitamin C
to get your day going right!

1. In a blender, combine the mandarin oranges, orange juice, and lemon juice. Purée until smooth.

2. Add the milk, whey powder, sugar, and ice cubes to the blender and process until smooth and creamy.

3. Pour into two tall glasses and enjoy.

5. Breads, Muffins, and Biscuits

Who doesn't love the lush texture of a muffin, the crisp crust of focaccia, or the flakiness of a hot biscuit? Thankfully, following a pH-balanced lifestyle doesn't mean that you can't enjoy these wonderful baked goods. Rather than deny you your favorite edible pleasures, this cookbook is designed to let you enjoy them without the harmful effects that typical ingredients have on your system. While some of the following recipes may not feature exactly the same components as their traditionally made counterparts, the taste of these scrumptious treats has definitely not been affected.

You'll be thrilled to bite into a warm scone or catch the scent of fresh bread from scratch. There is nothing quite like savoring a biscuit straight out of the oven or the satisfaction of preparing a veggie sandwich with a tortilla that you made yourself. Over the course of this chapter, you'll learn how to partake of each of these wonderful moments without worrying about your pH level going haywire.

YEAST-FREE SPELT BREAD

This hearty bread is as delicious plain as it is toasted. While the lack of yeast makes the bread significantly less acidifying than most other varieties, it also makes for a slightly heavier loaf than you may be used to eating. When slicing yeast-free bread, be sure to use a sharp non-serrated knife.

YIELD: TWO 9-X-5-INCH LOAVES

• • • • • • • • •

8 cups light spelt flour

¹/₂ cup raw sesame seeds

2 teaspoons baking powder

¹/₂ teaspoon sea salt

4¹/₄ cups unsweetened almond milk

1 tablespoon molasses

1. Preheat the oven to 350°F. Lightly coat two 9-x-5-inch loaf pans with vegetable oil or clarified butter and set aside.

2. In a large bowl, whisk together the flour, sesame seeds, baking powder, and salt. Make a well in the center of the dry ingredients

3. Quickly stir the milk and molasses into the dry ingredients until a stiff batter forms.

4. Spoon the batter evenly into the prepared loaf pans. Knock each pan on the counter to remove any large air pockets. Cover the pans with aluminum foil to keep the top of each loaf from splitting.

5. Bake for 40 minutes. Remove the pans from the oven, discard the foil, and return the pans to the oven for 30 additional minutes, or until a toothpick inserted in the center of the bread comes out clean.

6. Let the loaves cool in the pans for at least 5 minutes before transferring them to a cooling rack.

BREAD MACHINE SPELT BREAD

While this recipe contains yeast, it is much more alkaline than regular homemade or store-bought bread. If you have yeast-related health problems, simply make the Yeast-Free Spelt Bread (above) instead.

YIELD: ONE 2-POUND LOAF

• • • • • • • • •

1 cup unsweetened almond milk

¹/₂ cup water

2 tablespoons light olive oil

2 tablespoons Sucanat sugar

1 teaspoon sea salt

4 cups light spelt flour, or 2 cups light spelt flour and 2 cups whole spelt flour (in that order)

1¹/₂ teaspoons bread machine yeast

1. Place all of the ingredients in the pan of the bread machine in the order listed.

2. Select Quick Bread Cycle (which has only 2 risings) and press Start.

RUSTIC FOCACCIA BREAD

*This recipe is incredibly easy and does not use any acidifying yeast.
To add a zing to your bread, pull it out a few minutes early, top it
with grilled vegetables, and pop it back in the oven for the remaining
baking time. Whether plain or jazzed up, you're going to love it!*

1. Preheat the oven to 425°F. Lightly coat a 9-x-13-inch baking dish
with vegetable oil or clarified butter, or line it with parchment paper, and
set aside.

2. In a large bowl, whisk together the flour, baking powder, and salt.
Make a well in the center of the dry ingredients

3. In a small bowl, combine the water and $1/2$ teaspoon of the oil. Stir
until well blended and pour the liquid into the dry ingredients. Mix
quickly with a spoon until a sticky and elastic dough forms.

4. Lightly coat your hands with oil. Place the dough on a floured surface and knead it until it forms a ball.

5. Place the dough on the prepared baking sheet and spread it out with
your fingers until it is about $1/2$-inch thick.

6. Rub the top and sides of the dough with the remaining tablespoon of
oil. Season it with the cheese, rosemary, and garlic salt.

7. Bake for 25 minutes, or until the bread is golden brown.

8. To include additional toppings, remove the dough from the oven
after only 20 minutes of baking, sprinkle the toppings over the dough,
and return it to the oven for 5 additional minutes.

9. Let the bread cool for at least 5 minutes before transferring it to a
cooling rack.

**YIELD: ONE 9-X-13-INCH
DISH**

• • • • • • •

2 cups light spelt flour

2 teaspoons baking powder

$1/2$ teaspoon sea salt

1 cup tepid water

1 tablespoon plus $1/2$
teaspoon extra virgin
olive oil, divided

1 tablespoon grated
Parmesan cheese

1 teaspoon crushed
dried rosemary

$1/2$ teaspoon garlic salt

KAMUT FLAT BREAD

This is one of my favorite breads. It is quick and easy to make, and goes great with dips and spreads.

1. Preheat the oven to 450°F. Lightly coat a 9-x-13-inch baking sheet with vegetable oil or clarified butter, or line it with parchment paper, and set aside.

2. In a small bowl, combine the milk and vinegar. Stir until well blended and let the mixture sit while you prepare the dry ingredients.

3. In a medium-sized bowl, whisk together the flour, sugar, baking powder, and salt. Make a well in the center of the dry ingredients.

4. Add the oil to the milk and vinegar and stir until well blended.

5. Add the wet ingredients to the dry ingredients and mix quickly with a spoon until a smooth but stiff dough forms.

6. Lightly coat your hands with oil. Place the dough on the prepared baking sheet and pat it into a round loaf that measures about 8 inches in diameter and $1/2$ inch thick. Prick the top of the loaf with a fork.

7. Bake for 10 to 12 minutes, or until the loaf is golden brown. Cut it into wedges while still warm and serve.

YIELD: ONE 8-INCH ROUND LOAF

• • • • • • •

1 cup unsweetened almond milk

1 tablespoon apple cider vinegar

2 cups kamut flour

1 tablespoon Sucanat sugar

2 teaspoons baking powder

$1/2$ teaspoon sea salt

2 tablespoons olive oil

Top Ten Alkalizing Foods

With so many delicious alkalizing foods from which to choose, wading through all the options may seem a bit overwhelming. Here's a quick top-ten list for those times when you're looking for the best of the best.

1. Asparagus	6. Kale
2. Celery	7. Kelp
3. Chestnuts	8. Miso
4. Citrus fruit	9. Onions
5. Collard greens	10. Sweet Potatoes

MULTIGRAIN TORTILLAS

Use these tortillas to make burritos, tacos, or even as sandwich wraps.
They are absolutely delicious when stuffed with your choice of roasted veggies,
a little Almond Mayo (page 78), and a dollop of Pumpkinseed Pesto (page 94).

1. In a large bowl, whisk together the flour and salt.

2. Add the butter to the flour, mixing it in with a fork, pastry cutter, or even your fingertips.

3. Gradually add the water to the flour mixture, mixing it in with a spoon until a sticky dough forms.

4. Lightly coat your hands with oil. Place the dough on a floured surface and knead it for 2 to 3 minutes, or until firm.

5. Cover the dough and allow it to rest for 15 minutes.

6. Divide the dough into 12 balls of equal size. Cover and allow them to rest for 45 minutes to 1 hour.

7. On a floured surface, use a rolling pin to roll each ball into as thin a circle as possible (about $1/8$ inch thick).

8. Heat a dry 12-inch cast-iron skillet over medium-high heat until a drop of water sputters on the surface.

9. Place one of the tortillas in the pan and cook for about 2 minutes, or until the dough looks dry and brown spots begin to form on the bottom of the tortilla. The dough should puff up to about l/2 inch thick.

10. Turn the tortilla over and cook for 1 to 2 minutes. Make sure it does not become crisp from overcooking.

11. Keep the cooked tortillas wrapped in waxed paper or a damp dish towel until they are ready to eat.

YIELD: TWELVE 5-INCH TORTILLAS

• • • • • • • •

2 cups light spelt flour, or 1 cup light spelt flour and 1 cup kamut or amaranth flour

1 teaspoon sea salt

3 tablespoons clarified butter

$3/4$ cup warm water

HELPFUL TIP

You can flavor these tortillas with any combination of spices. When experimenting with seasonings, mix dry spices into the dry ingredients and fresh seasonings into the wet ingredients. I often make green wraps by adding a couple of tablespoons of unsweetened greens powder into the recipe. You can also make pesto wraps by substituting 2 tablespoons of Pumpkinseed Pesto (page 94) for the equivalent amount of clarified butter, or add a little dried tomato powder to make tomato-flavored wraps.

HERBED SPELT BISCUITS

*Not only are these biscuits fast to bake and so yummy, they also
have much less fat than your average baked good. Serve them
with a steaming hot bowl of vegetable soup or topped with a small
amount of cream cheese and a side of marinated vegetables.*

1. Preheat the oven to 425°F. Lightly coat a 9-x-13-inch baking sheet
with vegetable oil or clarified butter, or line it with parchment paper,
and set aside.

2. In a large bowl, whisk together the flour, chives, baking powder,
rosemary, thyme, and salt. Make a well in the center of the dry ingredients

3. In a medium-sized bowl, combine the water and butter. Stir until
well blended.

4. Add the wet ingredients to the dry ingredients. Mix well with a
spoon until the dough holds together (about 10 to 12 strokes). Spoon
12 circular mounds on the prepared baking sheet.

5. Bake for 10 to 12 minutes, or until the bottoms of the biscuits are
golden brown. Serve warm with Clarified Butter (page 19).

YIELD: 12 BISCUITS
. . . .

2 cups light spelt flour

$1/4$ cup finely chopped
fresh chives

$1 1/2$ tablespoons baking powder

$1/2$ teaspoon dried rosemary

$1/2$ teaspoon dried thyme

$1/4$ teaspoon sea salt

$7/8$ cup tepid water

3 tablespoons melted clarified
butter or olive oil

SPELT SCONES WITH CURRANTS

*Instead of grabbing a coffee and donut during your morning break,
sit down with a lovely cup of herbal tea and one of these scrumptious
scones. You'll thank yourself for the rest of the day!*

1. Preheat the oven to 400°F degrees. Lightly coat a 9-x-13-inch baking sheet with vegetable oil or clarified butter, or line it with parchment paper, and set aside.

2. In a large bowl, whisk together the flour, currants, baking powder,
and salt.

3. Cut the butter into the dry ingredients and mix well with a fork
until crumbly. Make a well in the center of the dry ingredients.

YIELD: 8 LARGE SCONES
. . . .

3 cups light spelt flour

$2/3$ cup currants

4 teaspoons baking powder

$1/4$ teaspoon sea salt

6 tablespoons chilled
clarified butter

1 cup unsweetened
almond milk

$1/3$ cup rice syrup

4. In a medium-sized bowl, combine the milk and rice syrup. Stir until well blended.

5. Add the wet ingredients to the dry ingredients and mix with a spoon just until combined. Do not overmix. Let the dough rest for 5 minutes.

6. On the prepared baking sheet, pat or roll out the dough into a $^3/_4$-inch thick round. With a sharp knife, score the round into 8 wedges.

7. Bake for 18 to 20 minutes, or until the edges start to brown and a toothpick inserted in the center of the dough comes out clean.

8. Cut along the score marks and place the individual scones on a wire rack to cool for a few minutes. Serve warm.

RAISIN ZUCCHINI MUFFINS

These muffins are incredibly good and very filling. No one will know that they are made with healthy alkaline ingredients. For a change of pace, add a different fruit, such as finely chopped apricots, or sprinkle in a few sunflower seeds or chopped almonds.

1. Preheat the oven to 375°F. Lightly coat a 12-cup muffin pan with vegetable oil or clarified butter, or use a silicone muffin pan or paper liners, and set aside.

2. In a large bowl, combine the water and flaxseed. Stir until well blended and let sit for 10 minutes. Add the milk, raisins, zucchini, molasses, sugar, applesauce, and butter. Stir until well blended.

3. In another large bowl, whisk together the flour, baking powder, cinnamon, baking soda, and salt. Make a well in the center of the dry ingredients.

4. Add the wet ingredients to the dry ingredients and mix well with a spoon just until combined.

5. Divide the batter evenly among the prepared muffin cups. Bake for 35 minutes, or until a toothpick inserted in the center of a muffin comes out clean.

6. Let the muffins cool in the pan for no more than 2 minutes before transferring them to a cooling rack.

YIELD: 12 MUFFINS

• • • • • • •

6 tablespoons water

2 tablespoons ground flaxseed

1 $^1/_2$ cups unsweetened almond milk

1 $^1/_2$ cups dark raisins

1 $^1/_2$ cups grated zucchini

$^1/_3$ cup molasses

$^1/_3$ cup Sucanat sugar

$^1/_4$ cup unsweetened applesauce

$^1/_4$ cup melted clarified butter

3 cups light spelt flour

1 tablespoon baking powder

2 teaspoons ground cinnamon

1 teaspoon baking soda

$^1/_2$ teaspoon sea salt

OATMEAL BANANA MUFFINS

*Can't decide between oatmeal cookies and banana bread?
Now you don't have to! These amazingly tasty
muffins give you the best of both worlds.*

YIELD: 12 MUFFINS

2 cups light spelt flour

I cup old-fashioned rolled oats

1/2 cup Sucanat sugar

I tablespoon baking powder

I teaspoon baking soda

1/4 teaspoon sea salt

I cup unsweetened vanilla-flavored almond milk

I cup mashed banana

1/2 cup unsweetened applesauce

1/4 cup clarified butter

1. Preheat the oven to 400°F. Lightly coat a 12-cup muffin pan with vegetable oil or clarified butter, or use a silicone muffin pan or paper liners, and set aside.

2. In a medium-sized heatproof bowl, whisk together the flour, oats, sugar, baking powder, baking soda, and salt. Make a well in the center of the dry ingredients.

3. In a large bowl, combine the milk, banana, applesauce, and butter. Mix well with a spoon until blended.

4. Add the dry ingredients to the wet ingredients and mix just until combined.

5. Divide the batter evenly among the prepared muffin cups. Bake for 25 minutes, or until a toothpick inserted in the center of a muffin comes out clean.

6. Let the muffins cool in the pan for no more than 2 minutes before transferring them to a cooling rack.

OJ GOJI MUFFINS

*If you love cranberry muffins but want to avoid their high acidity,
try this recipe. By substituting dried goji berries for cranberries,
you'll get the tangy flavor you expect while alkalizing your snack!*

YIELD: 12 MUFFINS

I cup boiling water

I cup dried goji berries

I cup old-fashioned rolled oats

2 tablespoons ground flaxseed

1 1/2 cups light spelt flour

1 1/2 cups oat flour

3/4 cup Sucanat sugar

2 teaspoons baking powder

I teaspoon baking soda

1/2 cup unsweetened almond milk

1/2 cup unsweetened applesauce

1/2 cup melted clarified butter

Juice of I orange

Zest of I orange

1. Preheat the oven to 375°F. Lightly coat a 12-cup muffin pan with vegetable oil or clarified butter, or use a silicone muffin pan or paper liners, and set aside.

2. In a medium-sized heatproof bowl, combine the boiling water, goji berries, oats, and flaxseed. Stir until well blended well and let sit for 10 minutes.

3. In a large bowl, whisk together the flours, sugar, baking powder and baking soda. Make a well in the center of the dry ingredients.

4. In a small bowl, combine the milk, applesauce, butter, orange juice, and orange zest. Mix well with a spoon until blended. Add the mixture to the water.

5. Add the wet ingredients to the dry ingredients and mix just until combined.

6. Divide the batter evenly among the prepared muffin cups. Bake for 35 minutes, or until a toothpick inserted in the center of a muffin comes out clean.

7. Let the muffins cool in the pan for no more than 2 minutes before transferring them to a cooling rack.

APPLE OAT AND NUT MUFFINS

These muffins are the perfect treat when you're stuck inside on a cold day. The delicious combination of apples, cinnamon, and pumpkin seeds makes you feel safe, warm, and satisfied.

1. Preheat the oven to 400°F. Lightly coat a 12-cup muffin pan with vegetable oil or clarified butter, or use a silicone muffin pan or paper liners, and set aside.

2. In a large bowl, whisk together the flour, oats, sugar, baking powder, cinnamon, and baking soda. Make a well in the center of the dry ingredients.

3. In a medium-sized bowl, combine the apples, milk, pumpkin seeds, applesauce, butter, and rice syrup. Mix well with a spoon until blended.

4. Add the wet ingredients to the dry ingredients and mix just until combined

5. Divide the batter evenly among the prepared muffin cups. Bake for 15 to 20 minutes, or until a toothpick inserted in the center of a muffin comes out clean.

6. Let the muffins cool in the pan for no more than 2 minutes before transferring them to a cooling rack.

YIELD: 12 MUFFINS

$1\frac{1}{3}$ cups light spelt flour

1 cup old-fashioned rolled oats

$\frac{1}{2}$ cup Sucanat sugar

1 tablespoon baking powder

$1\frac{1}{2}$ teaspoons ground cinnamon

1 teaspoon baking soda

1 cup finely chopped peeled apples

$\frac{1}{2}$ cup unsweetened almond milk

$\frac{1}{2}$ cup finely chopped and shelled raw pumpkin seeds, unsalted cashews, or macadamia nuts

$\frac{1}{4}$ cup unsweetened applesauce

$\frac{1}{4}$ cup melted clarified butter

$\frac{1}{4}$ cup rice syrup

CHOCOLATE SURPRISE MUFFINS

*These muffins are a delight for kids at lunchtime. They not only
have a wonderfully rich and chocolaty taste, but also contain
a delicious little coconut surprise buried in the middle.
Be sure to get your hands on one before they all get devoured!*

YIELD: 12 MUFFINS

1 ½ cups light spelt flour

1 ½ cups teff flour

⅔ cup Sucanat sugar

¼ cup organic cocoa

1 tablespoon baking powder

1 teaspoon baking soda

1 ½ cups unsweetened
vanilla-flavored almond milk

¼ cup clarified butter,
brought to room
temperature

¼ cup unsweetened
applesauce

COCONUT FILLING

½ cup unsweetened
flaked coconut

2 ounces cream cheese

2 tablespoons rice syrup

2 tablespoons egg substitute

½ teaspoon stevia (1 packet)

1. Preheat the oven to 400°F. Lightly coat a 12-cup muffin pan with
vegetable oil or clarified butter, or use a silicone muffin pan or paper liners, and set aside.

2. In a small bowl, combine all of the Coconut Filling ingredients and
mix well with a spoon until blended. Refrigerate and let sit while you
prepare the muffin batter.

3. To prepare the muffin batter, whisk together the flours, sugar, cocoa,
baking powder, and baking soda in a medium-sized bowl. Make a well
in the center of the dry ingredients.

4. In a small bowl, combine the milk, butter, and applesauce. Mix well
with a spoon until blended.

5. Add the wet ingredients to the dry ingredients and mix just until
combined.

6. Spoon out just enough batter to cover the bottom of each the prepared muffin cups. Add 1 teaspoon of Coconut Filling per cup and cover
evenly with the remaining batter.

7. Bake for 30 minutes, or until a toothpick inserted in the center of a
muffin comes out clean.

8. Let the muffins cool in the pan for no more than 2 minutes before
transferring them to a cooling rack.

ALMOND BUTTER AND JAM MUFFINS

If you are a peanut butter and jam sandwich lover, these muffins are bound to put a smile on your face. It's amazing how a little jam tucked into the center of each muffin makes them such a special treat. You'll feel like a kid again with just one bite.

1. Preheat the oven to 400°F. Lightly coat a 12-cup muffin pan with vegetable oil or clarified butter, or use a silicone muffin pan or paper liners, and set aside.

2. In a large bowl, combine the almond butter, egg substitute, and clarified butter. Mix well with a spoon until blended.

3. Add the sugar to the mixture and mix well again. Stir in the milk.

3. In a medium-sized bowl, whisk together the flour, baking powder, baking soda, and salt. Make a well in the center of the dry ingredients.

4. Add the dry ingredients to the wet ingredients and mix just until combined.

5. Spoon out just enough batter to cover the bottom of each of the prepared muffin cups. Add 1 teaspoon of jam per cup and cover evenly with remaining batter.

6. Bake for 15 minutes, or until a toothpick inserted in the center of a muffin comes out clean and they appear golden brown.

7. Let the muffins cool in the pan for no more than 2 minutes before transferring them to a cooling rack.

YIELD: 12 MUFFINS

• • • • • • • •

1 cup almond butter

$1/4$ cup egg substitute

2 tablespoons melted clarified butter

$1/2$ cup Sucanat sugar

1 cup unsweetened almond milk

$1 1/2$ cups light spelt flour

1 tablespoon baking powder

$1/2$ teaspoon baking soda

$1/4$ teaspoon sea salt

4 tablespoons fruit juice-sweetened raspberry or strawberry jam

"The superior man cultivates a friendly atmosphere, without being weak. He stands erect in the middle, without inclining to either side."

— Confucius, philosopher

SAVORY CHICKPEA FLOUR MUFFINS

These savory muffins are great as a snack alongside a hearty bowl of soup. Spread them with hummus or baba ganoush for a truly tasty and unique muffin experience!

YIELD: 12 MUFFINS

2 tablespoons finely chopped sun-dried tomatoes

1 tablespoon dried onion flakes

$7/8$ cup boiling water

$1\frac{1}{2}$ cups chickpea flour

$\frac{1}{2}$ cup light spelt flour

2 teaspoons baking powder

2 teaspoons dried basil

1 teaspoon Sucanat sugar

$\frac{1}{4}$ teaspoon sea salt

1 cup grated zucchini

$\frac{1}{4}$ cup egg substitute

1. Preheat the oven to 350°F. Lightly coat a 12-cup muffin pan with vegetable oil or clarified butter, or use a silicone muffin pan or paper liners, and set aside.

2. In a medium-sized heatproof bowl, soak the tomatoes and onion flakes in the boiling water for 15 minutes.

3. In a large bowl, whisk together the flours, baking powder, basil, sugar, and salt. Make a well in the center of the dry ingredients

4. Add the zucchini, egg substitute, and oil to the soaking water and stir until well blended. Make sure the water has cooled so that the egg substitute does not cook.

5. Add the wet ingredients to the dry ingredients and mix well with a spoon just until combined.

6. Divide the batter evenly among the prepared muffin cups. Bake for 15 to 20 minutes, or until a toothpick inserted in the center of a muffin comes out clean.

7. Let the muffins cool in the pan for no more than 2 minutes before transferring them to a cooling rack.

> "What lies behind us and what lies before us are tiny matters compared to what lies within us."
> — Ralph Waldo Emerson, author

3 tablespoons extra virgin olive oil

6. Snacks and Dips

Often taking a back seat to breakfast, lunch, and dinner, snacks are the unsung hero of the average day. Snacks satisfy our hunger between meals, giving us energy at those times when we need it while also boosting nutrition. Because store-bought treats are frequently packed with refined sugars and other acidifying ingredients, I have designed some pH-balanced options that you can easily make at home.

Whether you go for savory snacks or you want to satisfy a sweet tooth, the following recipes are sure to satisfy any craving. Featuring tasty bean dips, creamy vegetable dips, and hearty salsa, these dishes can be enjoyed at parties and get-togethers. If you're looking for a dessert treat to munch on while watching a movie at home, the sweet treats found in this chapter—with scrumptious flavors like lemon, chocolate, and coconut—are guaranteed to do the trick without causing acidifying dips in your pH level. All of these dishes tend to disappear quickly, though, so it may be wise to make double batches!

YIELD: 5 CUPS

• • • • • • • • • •

1 teaspoon ground coriander

1/2 teaspoon chili powder

1/2 teaspoon ground cumin

1/2 teaspoon garlic salt

1/4 teaspoon cayenne pepper

1/4 teaspoon ground cinnamon

1/4 teaspoon ground ginger

2 tablespoons light olive oil

2 cups whole almonds

2 cups pecan halves

1/2 cup shelled raw pumpkin seeds

1/2 cup shelled raw
sunflower seeds

1 tablespoon coarse sea salt

SPICED ROASTED NUT MIX

This snack will keep in airtight container for up to two weeks. Enjoy it yourself or give it as a gift in a parchment-lined box or an airtight jar.

1. Preheat the oven to 325°F. Line a 9-x-13-inch baking dish with parchment paper and set aside.

2. In a small bowl, whisk together the coriander, chili powder, cumin, garlic salt, cayenne pepper, cinnamon, and ginger. Set aside.

3. In an 8-inch nonstick skillet, heat the oil over low heat. Add the spice mixture and cook for 3 to 4 minutes, stirring often.

4. In a large bowl, combine the nuts and seeds. Add the spice mixture and toss well.

5. Spread the mixture over the prepared baking dish and bake for 15 minutes, shaking the dish every 5 minutes.

6. Sprinkle with the sea salt and a bit more garlic salt, if desired. Cool completely in the baking dish and serve.

YIELD: 1 1/2 CUPS

• • • • • • • • •

3 cups loosely packed cilantro
(about 1 large bunch)

3 scallions, coarsely chopped

1/4 cup light cream cheese,
brought to room temperature

1 cup mayonnaise (soy, egg,
and gluten-free) or Almond
Mayo (page 78)

1 tablespoon unsweetened
greens powder

1 teaspoon hot sauce (or
more to taste)

1/2 teaspoon sea salt

ZIPPY CILANTRO DIP

While the greens powder alkalizes this dip significantly, the cilantro, scallions, and hot sauce really give it a zip!

1. In food a processor, combine the cilantro and scallions. Process until well chopped.

2. Add the cream cheese, mayonnaise, greens powder, hot sauce, and salt to the food processor and process until smooth.

3. Transfer the dip to a bowl, cover, and refrigerate for at least 30 minutes before serving.

FRESH AVOCADO SALSA DIP

Not only are avocados alkalizing, they also promote healthy cholesterol levels and help to regulate blood pressure. So dip another chip and enjoy!

1. In a medium-sized bowl, combine the avocado, oil, lime juice, and salt. Mix gently with a spoon until blended.

2. Add the tomatoes, cilantro, onion, hot sauce, and chili powder to the avocado mixture and mix just until combined. Cover and refrigerate for at least 30 minutes before serving.

3. Serve with Spelt Tortilla Crisps (pg 61), Breakfast Burritos (pg 34), or over grilled chicken or seafood.

YIELD: 3 ½ CUPS
• • • • • • • •
2 ripe avocados, peeled, seeded, and diced

2 tablespoons extra virgin olive oil

1 tablespoon fresh lime juice

¼ teaspoon sea salt

2 small tomatoes, seeded and coarsely chopped

¼ cup finely chopped fresh cilantro

¼ cup finely chopped red onion

1 to 2 teaspoons hot sauce (optional)

½ teaspoon chili powder

WARM ARTICHOKE DIP

This dip is wonderfully simple and very tasty. In addition to alkalizing your system, artichokes provide an abundance of disease-fighting antioxidants.

1. Preheat the oven to 350°F.

2. In a medium-sized bowl, combine the artichoke hearts, mayonnaise, curd cheese, lemon juice, and garlic. Mix well with a spoon until blended.

3. Transfer the mixture to an 8-x-8-inch baking dish, sprinkle the Parmesan and paprika over top, and bake for 20 to 25 minutes, or until bubbly and lightly browned on top.

4. Let the dip cool slightly before serving. Serve with slices of toasted sprouted-grain or Spelt Bread (pg 44), or vegetable crudités.

YIELD: 3 ½ CUPS
• • • • • • • •
14-ounce can artichoke hearts, drained and chopped

1 cup mayonnaise (soy, egg, and gluten-free) or Almond Mayo (page 78)

½ cup grated curd cheese or mozzarella

2 tablespoons fresh lemon juice

1 clove garlic, pressed

2 tablespoons Parmesan cheese

Paprika

CHUNKY BLACK BEAN DIP

This dip is great to take to parties along with a basket of Spelt Tortilla Crisps (page 61). By using a soft cheese and throwing in a few additional vegetables, this recipe results in a bean dip that is much more alkaline than the traditional variety.

1. In a medium-sized bowl, partially mash the beans so that they remain a little chunky. Set aside.

2. Lightly coat a 10-inch skillet with vegetable oil or cooking spray and place over medium-low heat. Add the onion and cook, stirring regularly, for 4 minutes, or until translucent.

3. Add the peppers and garlic to the skillet and cook for 3 minutes.

4. Add the cumin, chili powder, salt, and hot sauce to the vegetables and cook for 2 minutes.

5. Add the cheese, mayonnaise, and lime juice to the beans and mix well with a spoon until blended. Add the cooked vegetables and mix just until combined.

6. Transfer the dip to a serving bowl, sprinkle with cilantro, and serve with Spelt Tortilla Chips (page 61).

YIELD: 4 1/2 CUPS

• • • • • • • •

15-ounce can black beans, rinsed and drained

1/2 cup chopped red onion

1/2 large green bell pepper, chopped

1/2 large red bell pepper, chopped

2 large cloves garlic, pressed

1 teaspoon ground cumin

1 teaspoon chili powder

1/2 teaspoon sea salt

Dash hot sauce (optional)

1/2 cup grated curd cheese or mozzarella

1/4 cup mayonnaise (soy, egg, and gluten-free) or Almond Mayo (page 78)

1 tablespoon fresh lime juice

1/4 to 1/2 cup finely chopped fresh cilantro

Top Ten Acidifying Foods

Although they are often seen as the bad guys, acidifying foods shouldn't be completely removed from your plate. Balance is the key to good health. The problem is that the North American diet has become so heavily acidic that certain highly acidifying foods should be reduced or, in some cases, avoided. Here's a top-ten list of the biggest no-nos when it comes to balancing your pH.

1. Artificial sweeteners
2. Black olives
3. Cheese
4. Coffee
5. Corn
6. Cranberries
7. Flour
8. Meat
9. Refined sugar
10. Soybeans

GREEN GARLIC CREAM CHEESE DIP

Delicious with crisp raw vegetables, baked potato chips, and brown rice crisps, this thick and garlicky dip also makes a great spread in sandwiches and wraps.

1. In a food processor or blender, combine all of the ingredients and process until well combined.

2. Transfer the dip to a bowl, cover, and refrigerate for at least 30 minutes before serving.

VARIATION

For Curry Dip, add 2 teaspoons ground coriander, $1/2$ teaspoon ground cumin, and $1/2$ teaspoon ground turmeric to give this dip Indian flair.

YIELD: 2 CUPS

• • • • • • • •

I cup light cream cheese, brought to room temperature

I cup mayonnaise (soy, egg, and gluten-free) or Almond Mayo (page 78)

I tablespoon unsweetened greens powder

I tablespoon lemon juice

2 teaspoons garlic dip mix, or 2 cloves garlic, pressed

Sea salt to taste

COCONUT COCOA BALLS

You can have *your cake and eat it too. Or rather, you can have your Coconut Cocoa Balls and eat* them *too. By combining alkalizing flavors with low-acid sweeteners, you can indulge your sweet tooth without upsetting your pH level.*

1. In a $2^1/_2$-quart saucepan, combine the rice syrup, sugar, milk, butters, and cocoa over medium-high heat. Cook, stirring regularly, until the mixture comes to a boil. Remove from the heat.

2. Add the oats, coconut, raisins, flaxseeds, sesame seeds, and sunflower seeds to the rice syrup mixture and stir until combined. Let sit until cool enough to handle. Roll into 1-inch balls.

3. Transfer the balls to a container, layering them between sheets of waxed paper, and refrigerate for at least 30 minutes before serving.

YIELD: 32 BALLS

• • • • • • • •

$1/2$ cup rice syrup

$1/2$ cup Sucanat sugar

$1/2$ cup almond milk

$1/4$ cup almond butter

$1/4$ cup clarified butter

$1/4$ cup cocoa

2 cups old-fashioned rolled oats

I cup unsweetened flaked coconut

I cup dark raisins

2 tablespoons flaxseeds

$1/4$ cup sesame seeds

$1/4$ cup shelled raw
sunflower seeds

BABA GANOUSH

*This traditionally Middle Eastern spread is made
with eggplants and lemon juice, which both alkalize it
and make it absolutely delicious.*

1. If using fresh eggplant, preheat the oven to 450°F.

2. Pierce the eggplants with a fork and place them on a 9-x-13-inch baking sheet lined with aluminum foil. Bake for 20 to 30 minutes, or until fork-tender. Cool for 10 minutes.

3. Cut each eggplant in half lengthwise and scoop the pulp out. Place the eggplant in a food processor and process it until smooth, or mash it by hand with a fork or potato masher.

4. Add the garlic, lemon juice, mayonnaise, tahini, salt, liquid smoke, and pepper to the eggplant and process or mix with a spoon until blended.

5. Slowly add 3 tablespoons of the oil to the eggplant and mix until creamy.

YIELD: $1 1/2$ CUPS
• • • • • • •

2 medium-sized eggplants,
or $1 1/2$ cups canned
roasted eggplant*

2 cloves garlic, pressed

$1/4$ cup fresh lemon juice

$1/4$ cup mayonnaise (soy, egg,
and gluten-free) or Almond
Mayo (page 78)

3 tablespoons tahini

$1/2$ teaspoon sea salt

$1/4$ teaspoon liquid smoke

Freshly ground black pepper
to taste

5 tablespoons extra virgin
olive oil, divided

$1/4$ cup chopped fresh parsley

Paprika as a garnish

HELPFUL TIP

I sometimes use canned roasted eggplant instead of fresh. The can may be marked "baba ganoush," but check the ingredients. If they include only eggplant and citric acid, it is really just a can of roasted eggplant and can be used for this recipe.

6. Transfer the Baba Ganoush to a shallow bowl, cover, and refrigerate for at least 2 hours. Sprinkle with the parsley and paprika, and drizzle the remaining 2 tablespoons of oil over top just before serving.

SPELT TORTILLA CRISPS

So, what do you do when you need something to scoop up all those delicious dips, but you don't want to ruin your pH-balance by using store-bought chips? Easy. You make these tasty little crisps.

1. In a large bowl or food processor, combine the flour, baking powder, and salt.

2. Add the oil and mix it into the dry ingredients with your fingertips, or process it with the food processor, until blended.

3. Work the water into the dough until a sticky ball forms. Cover the dough with plastic wrap and let it rest for at least 30 minutes.

4. Divide the dough into 6 to 8 balls. Cover them again with plastic wrap.

5. Lightly dust a counter or pastry board with spelt flour. Flatten the balls of dough with your hand one at a time, rolling them out into tortillas measuring about 6 to 7 inches in diameter and $1/8$ inch thick.

6. Preheat the oven to 350°F.

7. Heat a heavy 10-inch skillet (cast iron is best) over medium heat for 4 minutes, or until a drop of water spatters when it hits the surface. Cook the tortillas one at a time for 30 seconds, or until bubbles form. Flip the tortilla over, press down once or twice, and cook for about 30 seconds, or until golden. Do not overcook or they will be tough.

8. Lightly sprinkle the cooked tortillas with chili powder, cut them into wedges, and place them in a single layer on 9-x-13-inch baking sheets. Bake for 8 to 10 minutes, or until lightly toasted. Transfer the crisps to a bowl and serve with your choice of dip.

YIELD: 6 SERVINGS
• • • • • • •

2 cups light spelt flour

1 teaspoon baking powder

$1/2$ teaspoon sea salt

$1/4$ cup light olive oil

$1/2$ to $3/4$ cup warm water

Chili powder

"Happiness is not a matter of intensity but of balance, order, rhythm, and harmony."
— Thomas Merton, author

CRUNCHY GRANOLA BARS

Granola bars are the classic mid-afternoon snack. Instead of the store-bought kind that usually contains lots of refined sugars, throw one of these pH-balanced bars in your lunch box and you'll have something to look forward to that won't acidify your system.

1. Preheat the oven to 400°F.

2. Spread the oats, coconut, almonds, sunflower seeds, flaxseeds, pumpkin seeds, and sesame seeds evenly in a 9-x-13-inch baking dish. Bake, stirring occasionally, for 20 minutes, or until lightly toasted.

3. In a $1^1/_2$-quart saucepan, combine the rice syrup, molasses, sugar, butter, and salt over medium-low heat and cook for 10 minutes, stirring occasionally.

4. Transfer the oat mixture to a large bowl and add the dried fruit. Mix well with a spoon until combined.

5. Add the wet ingredients to the dry ingredients, stirring until the dry ingredients are completely coated.

6. Line an 11-x-13-inch glass baking dish with waxed or parchment paper. Lightly coat the paper with cooking spray and spread the granola evenly in the dish.

7. Place a piece of waxed or parchment paper on top of the baking dish and press down hard to compact the granola. Let cool completely.

8. Remove the top piece of paper and carefully turn the baking dish over on a large cutting board, allowing the solid block of granola to fall out. Peel off the rest of the paper. Using a large knife, slice the granola into 2-x-5-inch bars. Wrap the bars individually in waxed paper, or store them in an airtight container between sheets of waxed paper.

YIELD: 12 BARS

• • • • • • •

$2^1/_2$ cups old-fashioned rolled oats

I cup unsweetened shredded coconut

$1/_2$ cup slivered almonds

$1/_2$ cup shelled raw sunflower seeds

$1/_4$ cup flaxseeds

$1/_4$ cup shelled raw pumpkin seeds

$1/_4$ cup sesame seeds

$1/_2$ cup rice syrup

$1/_3$ cup molasses

$1/_3$ cup Sucanat sugar

$1/_4$ clarified butter

$1/_2$ teaspoon sea salt

I cup chopped unsulfured dried fruit (apples, apricots, goji berries, dark raisins, or other alkalizing fruit)

CHEWY SNACK SQUARES

These little morsels are truly a unique and delightful treat. The coconut and dried fruit add a nice flavor to the recipe, while also alkalizing it.

1. Coat a 9-x-9-inch glass baking dish with clarified butter and set aside.

2. In a medium-sized bowl, combine the cereal, coconut, and dried fruit. Mix well with a spoon and set aside.

3. In a $4^1/_2$-quart saucepan, combine the almond butter, rice syrup, clarified butter, and sugar over medium-low heat and cook for 2 to 3 minutes, stirring regularly, or until the mixture bubbles for at least 1 minute. Remove from the heat.

4. Immediately stir the dry ingredients into the almond butter mixture and mix well with a spoon until blended.

5. Transfer the mixture to the prepared baking dish and press it in an even layer.

6. Using a sharp knife, slice the mixture into 9 squares. Refrigerate until cool and serve.

VARIATION

To make Apple Cinnamon Squares, add 1 cup finely chopped dried apple and a teaspoon of ground cinnamon to the dry ingredients.

YIELD: 9 SQUARES

• • • • • • •

$2^1/_2$ cups puffed millet cereal or puffed brown rice cereal

1 cup unsweetened flaked coconut

1 cup chopped unsulfured dried fruit (cherries, goji berries, dark raisins, or other alkalizing fruit)

$^1/_2$ cup almond butter

$^1/_2$ cup rice syrup

1 tablespoon clarified butter

1 tablespoon Sucanat sugar

"Be moderate in order to taste the joys of life in abundance."

— Epicurus, philosopher

LEMON BARS

These snack bars are among my very favorite dessert treats. The lemon juice not only alkalizes the bars, but also makes them taste so tangy and good!

1. Preheat the oven to 300°F. Lightly coat a 9-x-9-inch baking dish with cooking spray and set aside.

2. In a large bowl, whisk together the cereal, oats, flours, and almonds. Set aside.

3. In a medium-sized bowl, combine the butter, rice syrup, lemon juice, sugar, and lemon zest. Mix well with a spoon until blended.

4. Add the wet ingredients to the dry ingredients and mix just until combined. Spread the mixture on the prepared baking sheet and press down evenly.

5. Bake for 15 to 20 minutes, or until the edges are golden brown. Slice into 24 bars and allow the bars to cool for 20 minutes, or until completely firm, before serving. Use a pizza cutter for easier slicing.

YIELD: 24 BARS

· · · · · · · ·

2 cups puffed rice or puffed millet cereal

1 cup old-fashioned rolled oats

1/2 cup light spelt flour

1/2 cup oat flour

1/3 cup ground almonds

1/3 cup melted clarified butter

1/3 cup rice syrup

1/3 cup fresh lemon juice

1/4 cup Sucanat sugar

Zest of 1 lemon

COCONUT MACAROONS

*Well now, who can resist a macaroon? Certainly not me.
The almond and coconut flavors make this recipe a hit every time.*

1. Preheat the oven to 325°F. Line a 9-x-13-inch baking sheet with parchment paper and lightly spray the paper with cooking spray.

2. In a medium-sized bowl, whisk together the coconut, sugar, flour, almonds, and salt. Set aside.

3. In a small bowl, combine the almond milk and rice syrup. Stir until well blended.

4. Add the wet ingredients to the dry ingredients and mix well with a spoon until blended.

5. Add the egg whites and mix just until blended. Let sit for about 5 minutes.

6. Drop 20 rounded teaspoonfuls on the prepared baking sheet, leaving 1/2 inch of room between the macaroons.

7. Bake for 10 to 15 minutes, or until the edges are golden brown. Cool the cookies completely on the baking sheet and serve. Transfer them to an airtight container for storage.

YIELD: 20 MACAROONS

· · · · · · ·

1 1/2 cups unsweetened flaked coconut

1/3 cup Sucanat sugar

2 1/2 tablespoons light spelt flour

2 tablespoons ground almonds

1/8 teaspoon sea salt

2 tablespoons unsweetened almond milk

2 tablespoons rice syrup

2 egg whites, brought to room temperature and lightly beaten

7. Soups

A fabulous way to get the recommended daily servings of vegetables is to have soup for lunch or as a first course to a meal. Most of these recipes are made on the stove, but they can also be prepared in a slow cooker, if you'd prefer. Just follow the manufacturer's instructions that came with your slow cooker.

Once you have become familiar with these soups, you will be able to adapt them to your own taste, adding and subtracting ingredients as you see fit. These recipes will also teach you about the ingredients you can use to make your own favorite home-made soups more alkalizing.

CREAM OF VEGETABLE SOUP

This soup is very easy to make and so very tasty. I use a frozen broccoli mix that includes green beans, onions, and mushrooms, but you can choose whichever vegetables you like.

1. In a 4$^1/_2$-quart saucepan, heat the butter over medium heat. Add the onion and sauté for 5 minutes, or until translucent.

2. Add the frozen vegetables, broth, and salt to the saucepan and cook uncovered, stirring occasionally, for 15 minutes, or until the vegetables are tender. Reduce the heat to low.

3. Add the milk, cream cheese, and Parmesan to the soup and stir until well blended.

4. Pour the soup into a blender, process until smooth, and return it to the saucepan, or use a hand blender directly in the saucepan. Reheat and serve.

YIELD: 8 SERVINGS

1 tablespoon clarified butter

1 large onion, coarsely chopped

2-pound bag frozen mixed vegetables

3 cups yeast-free organic vegetable broth

$^1/_2$ teaspoon sea salt, or 1 teaspoon miso dissolved in $^1/_4$ cup warm water

2 cups unsweetened almond milk

$^1/_3$ cup cream cheese

2 tablespoons grated Parmesan cheese

CREAMY KALE AND LENTIL SOUP

This soup is not only heart-warming, delicious, and alkalizing, it also freezes remarkably well. Just reheat it on your stove anytime you'd like to enjoy another steaming bowl.

1. In a 4$^1/_2$-quart saucepan, heat the oil over low heat. Add the garlic and cook for 3 minutes, or until fragrant.

2. Add the kale to the saucepan and cook for 3 minutes, stirring to coat it with the garlic and oil.

3. Add the water, bouillon, and salt to the saucepan and cook for 5 minutes, or until the kale is tender.

4. Add the lentils, milk, and cream cheese to the soup and stir until well blended. Add the Parmesan, if desired.

5. Pour the soup into a blender, process it until smooth, and return it to the saucepan, or use a hand blender directly in the saucepan. Reheat and serve.

YIELD: 12 SERVINGS

1 tablespoon light olive oil

3 large cloves garlic, pressed

8 cups coarsely chopped kale

3 cups water

1 yeast-free onion bouillon cube

$^1/_2$ teaspoon sea salt, or 1 teaspoon miso dissolved in $^1/_4$ cup warm water

19-ounce can lentils, drained and rinsed

2 cups unsweetened almond milk

$^2/_3$ cup cream cheese

¼ cup grated Parmesan cheese (optional)

ROASTED GARLIC SOUP

This recipe has become a hit at dinner parties.
It is fairly rich, so a little goes a long way.

1. Preheat the oven to 375°F.

2. Slice the garlic bulbs in half crosswise, exposing the cloves. In a 6-quart Dutch oven, combine the butter and garlic. Toss until the garlic is well coated.

3. Place the Dutch oven in the oven uncovered and roast the garlic, stirring occasionally, for 25 to 30 minutes, or until the cloves are soft and slightly browned. Remove the garlic from the oven and let it cool.

4. On a flat surface, press the garlic with the flat of a knife to remove the peel. Return the garlic to the Dutch oven.

5. Add the water, bouillon, and salt to the Dutch oven. Place the oven on the stove and bring to a boil over high heat. Reduce the heat to medium-low and simmer for 10 minutes.

6. Add the milk and cream cheese to the soup and stir until well blended. Pour the soup into a blender, process it until smooth, and return it to the Dutch oven, or use a hand blender directly in the Dutch oven. Reheat and serve piping hot with a bowl of croutons.

YIELD: 6 SERVINGS
· · · · · · · ·

4 large garlic bulbs, whole

2 tablespoons clarified butter

3 cups water

1 yeast-free onion bouillon cube

Sea salt to taste

2 cups unsweetened almond milk

¼ cup cream cheese

2 slices sprouted-grain or spelt bread, toasted, buttered, and cubed as a crouton garnish

HELPFUL TIP

You can avoid peeling the garlic by using a food mill, or moulinette. Once it is done roasting in the oven, let the unpeeled garlic cool and place it in a food mill. Process the garlic until pressed and ready to return to the dutch oven, and voilà! No peeling. Continue the recipe according to the instructions above to finish it.

CREAM OF CELERY SOUP

This is a hearty take on a classic soup. The potatoes turn this traditional starter into a main dish in the most satisfying way.

1. In a $4^1/_2$-quart saucepan, bring the broth to a boil over high heat. Add the celery, onions, and potatoes. Reduce the heat to medium-low, cover partially, and simmer, stirring occasionally, for 15 minutes, or until the potatoes are fork-tender.

2. Drain and transfer the cooked vegetables to a medium-sized bowl, reserving the broth in another medium-sized bowl.

3. Transfer the vegetables to a blender and process them until smooth, or use a hand blender directly in the bowl, adding the reserved broth as needed.

4. In the same saucepan, heat the butter over medium-low heat and whisk in the flour. Add the milk and stir until thickened.

5. Return the reserved broth to the saucepan and stir until well blended. Add the vegetables, salt, and pepper and stir until heated through. Garnish with a handful of the chopped celery leaves and serve.

YIELD: 8 SERVINGS

4 cups yeast-free organic vegetable broth

1 head of celery, trimmed of strings and tough joints, and coarsely chopped

3 medium-sized onions, peeled and diced

2 small potatoes, peeled and diced

1 tablespoon clarified butter

1 tablespoon light spelt flour

1 to $^1/_2$ cups unsweetened almond milk

$^1/_2$ teaspoon sea salt

Freshly ground black pepper to taste

Chopped celery leaves as a garnish

MISO SOUP

High in alkalizing minerals and low in calories, this dish is an excellent substitute for chicken soup and just as comforting when you're feeling under the weather!

1. In a $2^1/_2$-quart saucepan, bring the water to a boil over high heat. Reduce the heat to medium, add the wakame to the water, and simmer for at least 5 minutes.

2. Reduce the heat to low and add the rest of the ingredients to the saucepan. Stir well until the miso dissolves and serve. Be sure not to return the water to a boil, as the high temperature would ruin some of the miso's healthy properties and change the flavor of the soup.

YIELD: 4 SERVINGS

4 cups water

1 tablespoon shredded dried wakame (optional)

$^1/_2$ cup cooked spelt or brown rice noodles (optional)

$^1/_4$ cup finely chopped scallions

2 tablespoons light-colored miso

1 tablespoon tamari

1 clove garlic, pressed

$^1/_2$ teaspoon sesame oil

Pumpkin Ginger Pear Soup

Flavorful and spicy, this soup is great for lunch or as a tasty meal starter.

1. Drain and coarsely chop the pears, reserving the juice in a small bowl. Set aside.

2. In a 4$\frac{1}{2}$-quart saucepan, heat the butter over medium heat. Add the onion and sauté for 5 minutes, or until translucent.

3. Add the pears, ginger, and garlic to the saucepan and stir fry for 2 minutes.

4. Add the reserved pear juice, water, pumpkin, and salt to the saucepan. Reduce the heat to medium-low and simmer uncovered for 10 minutes, stirring occasionally.

5. Pour the soup into a blender, process it until smooth, and return it to the saucepan, or use a hand blender directly in the saucepan.

6. Add the milk to the soup and stir until well blended. Reheat and serve garnished with toasted pumpkin seeds.

YIELD: 10 SERVINGS

14-ounce can unsweetened pears in juice

1 tablespoon clarified butter

1 large onion, coarsely chopped

2 tablespoons peeled and grated ginger root

2 cloves garlic, pressed

3 cups water

1$\frac{1}{2}$ cups canned unsweetened pumpkin purée

$\frac{1}{2}$ teaspoon sea salt

2 cups unsweetened almond milk

Toasted pumpkin seeds (optional)

Borscht

A yummy borscht is a great way to use up those delicious and alkalizing beets that have been sitting in your fridge.

1. In a 4$\frac{1}{2}$-quart saucepan, combine the broth, onions, and salt, and bring to a boil over high heat.

2. Add the potatoes, beets, and carrots to the saucepan. Return to a boil, reduce the heat to medium-low, and cover. Simmer, stirring occasionally, for 30 minutes, or until the potatoes are fork-tender.

3. Add the cabbage and $\frac{1}{2}$ cup of the dill to the saucepan and cook, stirring occasionally, for 15 minutes, or until the cabbage is tender. Add the vinegar and stir until well blended.

4. Top each portion with a tablespoon of yogurt and a sprinkle of the remaining $\frac{1}{4}$ cup of dill and serve.

YIELD: 6 SERVINGS

6 cups yeast-free organic vegetable broth

2 medium-sized onions, quartered

$\frac{1}{2}$ teaspoon sea salt

2 large potatoes, peeled and diced into $\frac{1}{2}$-inch cubes

4 large beets, peeled and coarsely chopped

4 medium-sized carrots, chopped

2 cups thinly sliced Savoy cabbage

$\frac{3}{4}$ cup finely chopped fresh dill, divided

3 tablespoons apple cider vinegar

$\frac{1}{2}$ cup plain nonfat yogurt

ROASTED VEGETABLE SOUP

*The roasted vegetables give this soup an unbelievably good
flavor that will surely make it a family favorite.*

1. Preheat the oven to 400°F.

2. In a large bowl, combine the cauliflower, potatoes, onions, bell pepper, zucchini, and oil. Toss well to coat. Transfer the vegetables to a 9-x-13-inch baking dish, sprinkle them with $\frac{1}{2}$ teaspoon of the salt, and place in the oven.

3. Roast the vegetables, stirring occasionally, for 40 to 50 minutes, or until the potatoes are fork-tender and the cauliflower is lightly browned around the edges.

4. In an 8-quart stockpot, combine the roasted vegetables, water, remaining $\frac{1}{2}$ teaspoon of salt, and bouillon over high heat. Bring to a boil, reduce the heat to medium-low, and simmer for 10 minutes, stirring occasionally.

5. Transfer half of the soup to a blender and process it until smooth, or transfer half of the soup to a separate bowl and process it with a hand mixer.

6. Return the blended portion of soup to the stockpot, add the milk, and stir until well blended. Heat throughout and serve.

HELPFUL TIP

Hate doing dishes? Toss the vegetables and oil together directly in the stockpot before transferring them to the roasting pan. That's one less dish to clean.

CREAM OF CARROT AND CORIANDER SOUP

Because this recipe features so many carrots, I strongly recommend that you buy the organic variety, which is alkalizing, rather than conventionally grown carrots, which are mildly acid-forming due to their high level of residual pesticides.

1. In a 4½-quart saucepan, heat ½ tablespoon of the butter over medium-high heat. Add the onions and garlic. Sauté for 5 minutes, or until translucent.

2. Add the carrots, coriander, and paprika to the saucepan and stir until well blended. Cover, reduce the heat to low, and cook for 5 minutes, stirring occasionally.

3. Add the broth to the saucepan, cover partially, and simmer, stirring occasionally, for 15 minutes, or until the carrots are tender.

4. Transfer the vegetables to a blender, process them until smooth, and return them to the saucepan, or use a hand blender directly in the saucepan.

5. In a 1½-quart saucepan, heat the remaining tablespoon of butter over medium-low heat. Add the flour and stir until well blended. Add the milk and stir until thickened. Add the mixture to the soup.

6. Add the cream, salt, and pepper to the soup and stir until well blended. Top with a sprinkle of parsley or cilantro and serve.

YIELD: 8 SERVINGS

· · · · · · ·

1½ tablespoons clarified butter, divided

2 medium-sized onions, coarsely chopped

2 large cloves garlic, coarsely chopped

8 medium-sized carrots, chopped

1 tablespoon ground coriander

1 teaspoon paprika

4 cups yeast-free organic vegetable broth

1 tablespoon light spelt flour

1 cup unsweetened almond milk

½ cup light cream

Sea salt to taste

Freshly ground pepper to taste

Chopped fresh parsley or cilantro as a garnish

> **"Every patient carries her or his own doctor inside."**
> **— Albert Schweitzer, theologian**

LEEK AND POTATO SOUP

Not only is this soup a classic, it is also practically acid-free. Perhaps that is why it has stood the test of time.

1. In a 4¹/₂-quart saucepan, heat the butter over medium-low heat. Add the leeks and onion. Cover and cook, stirring occasionally, for 5 minutes, or until transparent.

2. Add the broth, potatoes, water, pepper, and salt to the saucepan. Cover and bring to a boil. Reduce the heat to medium-low and simmer, stirring occasionally, for 20 minutes, or until the potatoes are fork-tender.

3. Transfer half of the soup to a blender, process it until smooth, and return it to the saucepan, or lightly blend the soup directly in the saucepan with a hand blender, making sure to keep some of the vegetables intact.

4. Add the milk and cream to the soup and stir until well blended. Top with a sprinkle of parsley and serve.

YIELD: 6 SERVINGS

· · · · · · · · · ·

2 tablespoons clarified butter

2 large leeks, white and light green parts, thinly sliced

1 large onion, thinly sliced

3 cups yeast-free organic vegetable broth

4 medium-sized white potatoes, peeled and diced into 1-inch cubes

1 cup water

¹/₄ teaspoon freshly ground black pepper

Sea salt to taste

1 ¹/₂ cups unsweetened almond milk

¹/₂ cup light cream

Chopped fresh parsley as a garnish

CLAM CHOWDER

This is a much more alkaline version of the traditional clam chowder found here on the eastern shore of Nova Scotia. Because clams are a particularly low-acid shellfish, I make it often.

1. In an 8-quart stockpot, heat the butter over medium-low heat. Add the celery, leek, and onion. Cook, stirring occasionally, for 5 minutes, or until tender.

2. Add the potatoes, reserved clam liquid, and liquid smoke to the stockpot. Add water to cover the vegetables, cover, and cook, stirring occasionally, for 20 minutes, or until the potatoes are fork-tender.

3. Transfer 1 cup of the cooked potatoes to a medium-sized bowl, mash them, and return them to the stockpot.

4. Add the clams, milk, cream, salt, and pepper to the soup and stir until well blended. Increase the heat to medium-high and cook, stirring occasionally, for a few minutes, until heated through, making sure not to boil it. Top with a sprinkle of parsley and serve.

YIELD: 6 SERVINGS

· · · · · · · · · ·

2 tablespoons clarified butter

2 stalks celery, finely chopped

1 leek, finely chopped (optional)

1 large onion, finely chopped

4 medium-sized white potatoes, peeled and diced into 1-inch cubes

2 cans (5 ounces each) baby clams, drained, reserving liquid

¹/₄ teaspoon liquid smoke

1 ¹/₂ cups unsweetened almond milk

¹/₂ cup light cream

Sea salt to taste

Freshly ground pepper to taste

1 tablespoon chopped fresh parsley

CURRIED SQUASH SOUP

This hearty soup is a satisfying and alkalizing choice for lunch.
It tastes even better the next day, so be sure to save
a few ladles worth until then.

1. In a 4$\frac{1}{2}$-quart saucepan, heat the butter over medium heat. Add the onion and sauté for 5 minutes, or until translucent.

2. Add the garlic, coriander, cumin, and turmeric to the saucepan and stir fry for 1 minute.

3. Add the squash, water, and salt to the saucepan, cover partially, and cook, stirring occasionally, for 10 minutes, or until the squash is fork-tender. Reduce the heat to low.

4. Pour the soup into a blender, process it until smooth, and return it to the saucepan, or use a hand blender directly in the saucepan.

5. Add the milk and light cream to the soup and stir until well blended. Reheat, top with a sprinkle of the cilantro, and serve.

YIELD: 8 SERVINGS
• • • • • • • • • • •

1 tablespoon clarified butter

1 large onion, coarsely chopped

2 to 3 cloves garlic, pressed

2 teaspoons ground coriander

$\frac{1}{2}$ teaspoon ground cumin

$\frac{1}{2}$ teaspoon ground turmeric

6 to 8 cups peeled and diced butternut squash (about 3 pounds)

3 cups water or vegetable stock

$\frac{1}{2}$ teaspoon sea salt, or 1 teaspoon miso dissolved in $\frac{1}{4}$ cup warm water

1 cup unsweetened almond milk

$\frac{1}{2}$ cup light cream

$\frac{1}{4}$ cup chopped fresh cilantro as a garnish

HELPFUL TIP

Place the squash in boiling water for 5 minutes to make peeling easier. Or bake it in the oven and scoop the precooked squash into the soup before processing it with a blender.

BLENDED PARSNIP SOUP WITH HARISSA

*After my friend Sandra served this soup at one of my get-togethers,
I begged for the recipe. I love it not only for its amazing taste,
but also because parsnips are very alkalizing!*

1. In a $4^1/_2$-quart saucepan, melt the butter over medium-high heat. Add the onions and garlic. Sauté for 5 to 7 minutes, or until translucent.

2. Add the parsnips and potato to the saucepan and sauté for 3 to 5 minutes, stirring often.

3. Cover the parsnips and potato with the broth, reduce the heat to low, and cook, stirring occasionally, for 20 minutes, or until fork-tender. Let the soup cool slightly.

4. Transfer the soup to a blender, process it until smooth, and return it to the saucepan, or use a hand blender directly in the saucepan.

5. Add the milk, cream, and salt to the saucepan and stir until well blended. Cover and leave over low heat while you prepare the harissa.

6. To prepare the harissa, combine the caraway, coriander, and cumin in an 8-inch skillet over medium heat. Roast, stirring occasionally, for a few minutes, or until fragrant.

7. In a food processor, combine the oil, garlic, mint, salt, and chili flakes. Process until smooth. Add the roasted spices and process again until smooth. Transfer the harissa to a serving bowl.

8. Serve the parsnip soup along with the harissa, which can be drizzled on top according to preference.

9. Transfer the remaining harissa to an airtight container, drizzle a small amount of olive oil on top to keep it fresh, and place it in the refrigerator. The refrigerated harissa should keep for a month. Use the harissa on all kinds of veggie soups. It's also good on steamed carrots and other cooked vegetables.

YIELD: 6 SERVINGS

2 tablespoons clarified butter

3 medium-sized onions, coarsely chopped

2 cloves garlic, coarsely chopped

9 cups peeled and coarsely chopped parsnips (about 3 pounds)

1 large potato, peeled and diced

4 cups yeast-free organic vegetable broth or water

$1^1/_2$ cups unsweetened almond milk

$^1/_2$ cup light cream

Sea salt to taste

Harissa

1 tablespoon ground caraway seeds

1 tablespoon ground coriander

2 teaspoons ground cumin

$^1/_2$ cup extra virgin olive oil

4 cloves garlic

1 tablespoon dried mint

1 teaspoon sea salt

$^1/_8$ teaspoon chili flakes (optional)

INDIAN LENTIL SOUP

This recipe is adapted from a soup found in one of my favorite Indian restaurants. It took quite a while for me to perfect it, but it has become a fantastically delicious way to warm up on a chilly day.

1. In a $4^1/_2$-quart saucepan, heat the butter over medium heat. Add the cumin seeds, stirring constantly. Once they begin to pop and sizzle, add the onion and cook just until golden brown. Do not overcook.

2. Add the garlic, turmeric, and cayenne pepper to the saucepan. Cook for 2 minutes, stirring occasionally.

3. Add the ginger and coriander to the saucepan. Cook for 1 minute, stirring occasionally.

4. Add the water and lentils to the saucepan. Cover partially, reduce the heat to low, and cook, stirring occasionally, for 30 minutes, or until the lentils are very soft.

5. Stir the cooked lentils to blend them slightly, or use a hand blender for 1 minute.

6. Add the milk and salt to the soup and stir until blended and heated through. Top with cilantro and serve.

YIELD: 6 SERVINGS
• • • • • • • •

1 tablespoon clarified butter

1 teaspoon cumin seeds

1 large onion, finely chopped

3 cloves garlic, pressed

$1/_2$ teaspoon ground turmeric

$1/_8$ teaspoon ground cayenne pepper

1 tablespoon peeled and minced ginger root

2 teaspoons ground coriander

3 cups water

1 cup yellow lentils

1 cup unsweetened almond milk

$1/_2$ teaspoon sea salt

Chopped fresh cilantro as a garnish

Ionized Water

While eating alkalizing foods is the best way to fight acidosis, sometimes you need a little extra help. Because tap water is such a common element in cooking (particularly in soups) but also generally acidic, alkalizing it can be beneficial to your overall pH balance. Perhaps the best way to alkalize your water is by using a water ionizer.

A water ionizer is a filtration device that usually sits on your countertop. Tap water is run through the device, which uses an electrical current to create a chemical reaction, making the expelled water more alkaline. While these devices usually have settings that can make your water highly alkaline, simply getting your water back to its natural pH of about 7, or neutral, is all you need to do. As a bonus, many ionizers include a carbon filter, which eliminates a number of impurities that are commonly found in local water supplies.

YIELD: 12 SERVINGS

1 cup red lentils

½ cup Basmati rice

¼ cup clarified butter

2 large onions, finely chopped

2 stalks celery, finely chopped

2 carrots, chopped

4 cloves garlic, minced

2 teaspoons peeled and grated ginger root

2 teaspoons ground coriander

1½ teaspoons ground turmeric

1 teaspoon ground cumin

½ teaspoon ground cinnamon

4 green cardamom pods, bruised,
or ½ teaspoon ground cardamom

½ teaspoon fennel seeds

¼ teaspoon chili powder (optional)

¼ teaspoon ground cloves

2 tablespoons light spelt flour

4 cups yeast-free organic vegetable broth

3 cups water

3 boneless and skinless chicken breast halves,
cut into 1-inch cubes (about 10 ounces)

2 large potatoes, peeled and diced

2 apples, peeled, cored, and chopped

Sea salt to taste

Freshly ground black pepper to taste

2 cups coconut milk

1 cup light cream

¼ cup chopped fresh cilantro (optional)

1 tablespoon lemon juice

MULLIGATAWNY SOUP

This aromatic soup can be served as a starter or a meal in itself, and is great at parties. Leftovers can be easily frozen and thawed at room temperature. When reheating, do not bring it to a boil. This recipe can be halved, using the same cooking times.

1. Soak the lentils and rice in warm water for 20 minutes. Drain well and set aside.

2. In a 6-quart stockpot, combine the butter, onions, celery, and carrots over medium heat. Sauté, stirring often, for about 5 minutes, or until the onions are translucent.

3. Add the garlic, ginger, coriander, turmeric, cumin, cinnamon, cardamom, fennel, chili powder, and cloves to the stockpot. Cook, stirring often, for 2 minutes.

4. Sprinkle the flour evenly over the soup and cook, stirring well to avoid any lumps, for 1 minute.

5. Add the reserved lentils and rice, vegetable broth, water, chicken, potatoes, and apples to the stockpot. Stir well. Season with the salt and pepper, reduce the heat to medium-low, and let simmer for 30 minutes, or until the lentils and rice are soft.

6. Add the coconut milk, cream, cilantro, and lemon juice to the stockpot. Stir well until heated through. If using cardamom pods, discard them before serving.

8. Salads and Dressings

Salads are no longer just the appetizer that you have to get through on your way to the main meal. They are often the main dish themselves. And that is a great thing, because the more alkalizing salads you eat, the healthier you will be. It is that simple. Salads balance your pH level and supply you with the nutrients your body needs to function at its best.

This chapter begins with several versatile alkalizing dressings and continues with recipes for entire salads. These recipes range from simple mixed salad greens to heartier dishes that feature out-of-the-ordinary options such as rice, quinoa, sweet potato, shrimp, oranges, and beets. Some are wonderful starters, while others are so chocked full of vegetables that they deserve the starring role in your meal plan. Whenever you eat one, salad will never be boring again.

DRESSINGS

LEMON POPPY SEED DRESSING

YIELD: 1 1/4 CUPS

• • • • • • • •

3/4 cup light olive oil

1/4 cup fresh lemon juice

2 tablespoons mayonnaise (soy, egg, and gluten-free), or Almond Mayo (page 78)

1 tablespoon poppy seeds

2 teaspoons Sucanat sugar

1/2 teaspoon sea salt

Light and tangy, this dressing is great when you want something different on your salad. The lemon juice gives the dressing a zing and also alkalizes it.

1. In a large bowl, whisk together all of the ingredients until emulsified and creamy.

2. Store the dressing in an airtight container and refrigerate for up to 1 week.

ALMOND MAYONNAISE

YIELD: 2 CUPS

• • • • • • • •

1/2 cup ground blanched almonds or almond flour

1/2 cup water

3/4 teaspoon sea salt

1/2 teaspoon dry mustard

1/8 teaspoon paprika

3/4 cup light olive oil

1/4 cup flaxseed oil

2 tablespoons apple cider vinegar

Packed with protein and omega fatty acids, this mayo is one of the staples of my diet. Use it as a base for salad dressings or spread it on a chicken sandwich. It has all the flavor of traditional mayo without the acidifying properties.

1. Place the ground almonds in a food processor and process for 1 minute, or until they are as finely ground as flour. If using almond flour instead, add it to the food processor.

2. Add the water, salt, mustard, and paprika to the processor and process until well blended.

3. In a small measuring cup, combine the oils. Slowly add the oils to the processor, processing at low speed until blended.

4. Scrape down the sides of the processor, add the vinegar, and continue to process the mixture for 1 to 2 minutes, or until thickened.

5. Transfer the mayo to an airtight container and refrigerate for at least 30 minutes before using. Store it in the refrigerator for up to 2 weeks, or freeze it in freezer bags for up to 3 months.

OMEGA SALAD DRESSING

This simple dressing is a delicious way to get your omega fatty acids and alkalize your system at the same time.

1. In a large bowl, whisk together all of the ingredients until emulsified and creamy.

2. Store the dressing in an airtight container and refrigerate for up to 1 week.

VARIATION

Add 1 tablespoon unsweetened greens powder for an even more alkalizing dressing, or make an Italian-style dressing by adding 1 to 2 teaspoons ground basil or oregano.

> **YIELD: 1 ¼ CUPS**
>
> ¾ cup extra virgin olive oil
>
> ¼ cup flaxseed oil
>
> 3 tablespoons apple cider vinegar
>
> 2 tablespoons mayonnaise (soy, egg, and gluten-free) or Almond Mayo (page 78)
>
> 1 small clove garlic, pressed
>
> ½ teaspoon sea salt
>
> Freshly ground black pepper to taste

GREEN GODDESS DRESSING

This very rich salad dressing is best served on a bed of mixed salad greens with chunks of fresh tomatoes.

1. In a food processor, combine all of the ingredients and process until smooth. Add a little water if the dressing is too thick.

2. Store the dressing in an airtight container and refrigerate for up to 1 week.

> **YIELD: 1 CUP**
>
> ½ small avocado, peeled and pitted
>
> ¼ cup mayonnaise (soy, egg, and gluten-free) or Almond Mayo (page 78)
>
> ¼ cup chopped fresh chives or minced scallions
>
> ¼ cup chopped fresh parsley
>
> 1 tablespoon unflavored greens powder
>
> 1 tablespoon fresh lemon juice
>
> 1 large clove garlic, pressed
>
> 1 teaspoon anchovy paste
>
> Sea salt to taste
>
> Freshly ground black pepper to taste

SALADS

CAESAR SALAD

A friend of mine serves his Caesar salad this way. While it may seem strange at first, it is very rewarding to slice bite-sized portions for yourself as you eat this delicious dish.

YIELD: 6 SERVINGS

• • • • • • • • • •

$^3/_4$ cup extra virgin olive oil

3 large cloves garlic, thinly sliced

4 slices sprouted-grain bread sliced into $^1/_2$-inch cubes

Juice of 1 medium-sized lemon

$^1/_8$ cup egg substitute

2 teaspoons apple cider vinegar

$^1/_2$ teaspoon dry mustard

$^1/_2$ teaspoon sea salt

$^1/_2$ teaspoon freshly ground black pepper

3 small heads romaine lettuce

3 ounces finely shaved Parmesan cheese (about $^3/_4$ cup)

1. In a large glass measuring cup, combine the oil and garlic. Set aside for 1 hour.

2. In a 12-inch skillet, combine 2 tablespoons of the garlic oil with the bread. Toss to coat. Cook over medium-low heat, stirring constantly, until slightly toasted. Set aside.

3. Remove the garlic from the remaining oil and discard it. Add the lemon juice, egg substitute, vinegar, dry mustard, salt, and pepper to the measuring cup and whisk until emulsified and thickened.

4. Chop each head of lettuce in half lengthwise, making sure to leave the core attached so that the leaves remain attached on each half. On individual serving plates, arrange each half head of lettuce with the leaves facing upwards. Top each serving with an equal amount of dressing and $^1/_2$ ounce of Parmesan cheese. Add equal portions of the croutons and serve.

HELPFUL TIP

If you really love the taste of garlic, do Step One the night before and let the mixture sit in the refrigerator overnight. This will make the dressing extra garlicky.

BROCCOLI SOBA NOODLE SALAD

Although it is delicious cold, I usually toss the raw vegetables with the hot noodles and serve the dish slightly warm. Be sure to trim away the tough outer skin of the broccoli stems before chopping them.

1. In a large bowl, combine all of the ingredients except for the noodles. Toss well and set aside.

2. Break the noodles into 3-inch lengths, cook according to package directions, and drain. Cover the vegetables with the noodles, allowing them to steam the vegetables lightly for 3 minutes.

3. Toss well and serve. Refrigerate leftovers for up to 3 days.

YIELD: 6 SERVINGS

3 cups finely chopped broccoli

3 scallions, finely chopped

1 large carrot, grated

$1/4$ cup finely chopped cilantro

$1/4$ cup shelled raw pumpkin seeds

2 tablespoons extra virgin olive oil

2 tablespoons raw sesame seeds

2 tablespoons tamari

1 tablespoon grated ginger root

1 tablespoon sesame oil

Zest of 1 lemon

8 ounces soba noodles

TUSCAN KALE SALAD WITH SUNFLOWER SEEDS

It may be an unusual way to serve kale, but this salad is amazingly tasty and packed with nutrients.

1. Tightly roll up the kale leaves and chop them crosswise into $1/8$-inch strips. Chop the strips roughly.

2. In a large bowl, combine the kale, oil, and salt. Toss until the kale is well coated. Set aside for 10 minutes.

3. In an 8-inch skillet, toast the sunflower seeds over medium-low heat, stirring often, for 3 minutes, or until golden brown. Remove from the heat immediately.

4. Add the lemon juice, shallots, and pepper to the kale and toss well.

5. Top the salad with the toasted sunflower seeds and cheese. Serve.

YIELD: 6 SERVINGS

1 pound kale (preferably the Tuscan variety), stems and center leaves removed

$1/4$ cup extra virgin olive oil

$1/4$ teaspoon sea salt

$1/4$ cup shelled raw sunflower seeds

2 tablespoons fresh lemon juice

2 tablespoons finely chopped shallots

$1/4$ teaspoon freshly ground black pepper

1 cup grated curd cheese or mozzarella

BROCCOLI RAISIN SALAD

A classic salad turned alkaline, this dish will make your day. It's not your average, everyday salad, so make it when you're craving something out of the ordinary.

1. In a large bowl, combine the broccoli, raisins, carrot, onion, and sunflower seeds.

2. In a large measuring cup, combine the mayonnaise, sugar, and vinegar. Mix well with a spoon until blended.

3. Pour the dressing over the salad, toss well, and serve.

VARIATION

You can also use $^3/_4$ cup Lemon Poppy Seed Dressing (page 78) on this salad instead of the dressing suggested above.

YIELD: 6 SERVINGS

4 cups broccoli florets (about 2 heads)

1 cup dark raisins

1 large carrot, grated

$^1/_2$ cup finely chopped red onion

$^1/_2$ cup shelled raw sunflower seeds

Dressing

$^3/_4$ cup mayonnaise (soy, egg, and gluten-free) or Almond Mayo (page 78)

$^1/_4$ cup Sucanat sugar

2 tablespoons apple cider vinegar

FATTOUSH SALAD

I always order this salad at my favorite Lebanese restaurant. The finely chopped ingredients make it perfect for stuffing a wrap or topping an open-faced sandwich.

1. Preheat the oven to 400°F. Brush the flatbread rounds lightly with olive oil and place them on an 11-x-7-inch baking sheet. Toast the rounds in the oven for 10 minutes, or until they are slightly crisp. Set aside.

2. In a large bowl, combine the cucumber, parsley, onion, radishes, tomatoes, and bell pepper. Sprinkle the vegetables with the sumac.

3. In a small bowl, whisk together the lemon juice, oil, and salt until emulsified. Pour the dressing over the salad and toss well.

4. Coarsely tear the toasted flatbread rounds into pieces. Top the salad with the pieces of flatbread and serve.

YIELD: 6 SERVINGS

2 rounds sprouted-grain flatbread, or Multigrain Tortillas (page 47)

2 cups diced English cucumber

1 cup finely chopped fresh parsley

$^1/_2$ cup finely chopped red onion

5 medium-sized radishes, finely chopped

2 medium-sized tomatoes, seeded and finely chopped

1 green bell pepper, finely chopped

1 tablespoon sumac or Za'atar

$^1/_4$ cup fresh lemon juice

3 tablespoons extra virgin olive oil

$^1/_4$ teaspoon sea salt

QUINOA TABOULI SALAD

Traditionally a Lebanese dish, tabouli has become a favorite around the world. This recipe substitutes alkalizing quinoa for the highly acidifying bulgur wheat with which tabouli is normally made.

1. In a $2^1/_2$-quart saucepan, combine the quinoa and water over high heat and bring to a boil. Reduce the heat to low, cover, and simmer for 15 minutes, or until the quinoa completely absorbs the water and appears translucent, and a ring appears on the seed. Remove from the heat, fluff with a fork, and let cool.

2. In a large bowl, combine the tomatoes, cucumber, parsley, scallions, sunflower seeds, and mint.

3. In a small bowl, whisk together the oil, vinegar, garlic, and salt until emulsified. Pour the dressing over the vegetables and toss well.

4. Add the quinoa to the vegetables, toss well, and serve.

YIELD: 6 SERVINGS

. . . .

1 cup quinoa

2 cups water

4 medium-sized tomatoes, seeded and diced

1 medium-sized cucumber, peeled, seeded, and diced

1 cup finely chopped fresh parsley

1 cup finely chopped scallions

$1/_4$ cup sunflower seeds

1 tablespoon dried mint

3 tablespoons extra virgin olive oil

1 tablespoon apple cider vinegar

2 cloves garlic, pressed

$1/_2$ teaspoon sea salt

HELPFUL TIP

Always check the package of quinoa to see if the seeds have been rinsed. If they have not been rinsed, do so according to the directions on the package before cooking the quinoa.

SWEET POTATO SALAD

4 medium-sized sweet potatoes,
unpeeled and diced into 1-inch cubes

6 to 8 leaves kale, chopped,
stems removed

1 red bell pepper, chopped

$\frac{1}{2}$ cup shelled raw pumpkin seeds

2 tablespoons light olive oil

$\frac{1}{2}$ teaspoon sea salt

2 stalks celery, finely chopped

$\frac{1}{2}$ cup dark raisins

$\frac{1}{2}$ cup chopped scallions

$\frac{1}{4}$ cup extra virgin olive oil

2 tablespoons apple cider vinegar

1 tablespoon rice syrup

This dish is tasty and so good for you, especially when compared to standard potato salad, which is covered with acidifying mayonnaise. I bring it along to barbeques and never leave with leftovers. Sigh.

1. Preheat the oven to 425°F.

2. In a 9-x-13-inch roasting pan, combine the potatoes, kale, bell pepper, pumpkin seeds, light olive oil, and salt. Stir well. Bake for 15 minutes, or until the potatoes are fork-tender and golden brown. Let cool. Transfer the vegetables to a large bowl.

3. Add the celery, raisins, and scallions to the cooked vegetables and toss well to mix.

4. In a small bowl, whisk together the extra virgin olive oil, vinegar, and rice syrup until emulsified. Pour the dressing over the vegetables and toss well. Refrigerate until ready to serve.

FENNEL AND ORANGE SALAD

1 large fennel bulb

2 medium-sized oranges

$\frac{1}{2}$ red onion, thinly sliced

$\frac{1}{4}$ cup orange juice

2 tablespoons extra virgin olive oil

1 tablespoon apple cider vinegar

1 teaspoon poppy seeds

Sea salt to taste

6 cups mixed salad greens

If a beautiful spring day could be served in a bowl, it would taste like this light and sweet combination of fennel and oranges.

1. Quarter the fennel bulb, core it, and remove the feathery leaves of the stalks. Thinly slice the fennel and place it in a large bowl. Set aside.

2. Peel and remove the pith of the oranges. Quarter the oranges and slice the pieces crosswise. Add the oranges and onion to the fennel.

3. In a small bowl, whisk together the orange juice, oil, vinegar, poppy seeds, and salt until emulsified. Pour over the fennel and toss until coated.

4. Arrange 1 cup of the salad greens in each of 6 individual salad bowls. Top each bowl with a portion of the fennel mixture and serve.

SHRIMP-STUFFED AVOCADO SALAD

This salad proves that you can still enjoy your favorite foods as long as the meal itself is pH balanced. In this recipe, the alkalizing avocado and vegetables balance the highly acidifying shrimp in the most delightful way.

1. In a medium-sized bowl, combine the mayonnaise, light cream, cream cheese, pepper, and salt and mix well with a spoon until blended.

2. Add the shrimp, celery, cucumber, dill, and onion. Stir well, cover, and refrigerate for at least 1 hour.

3. Slice the avocados in half lengthwise and remove the pits. Spoon equal amounts of the shrimp mixture onto each avocado half. Sprinkle each avocado half with paprika.

4. Divide the salad greens equally among 4 serving plates. Place one stuffed avocado half on each plate and serve.

YIELD: 4 SERVINGS

2 tablespoons mayonnaise (soy, egg, and gluten-free) or Almond Mayo (page 000)

2 tablespoons light cream

1 tablespoon cream cheese, brought to room temperature

Pinch freshly ground black pepper

Pinch sea salt

$\frac{1}{2}$ cup cooked small shrimp

3 tablespoons finely diced celery

3 tablespoons finely diced cucumber

2 tablespoons chopped fresh dill or fresh parsley (optional)

1 teaspoon finely diced onion

2 avocados

Paprika

4 cups mixed salad greens

"The Tao is the One. From the One come yin and yang; from these two, creative energy (chi); from energy, ten thousand things, the forms of all creation. All life embodies yin and embraces yang, through their union achieving harmony."

— Lao Tzu, philosopher

YIELD: 4 SERVINGS
· · · · · · · ·

6 cups mixed baby salad greens

2 cups sliced strawberries

$\frac{1}{2}$ cup blueberries

$\frac{1}{2}$ cup unsweetened canned mandarin orange slices, drained

$\frac{1}{2}$ cup thinly sliced red onion

$\frac{1}{2}$ cup thinly sliced red bell pepper

$\frac{1}{4}$ cup shelled raw pumpkin seeds

Dressing

$\frac{1}{3}$ cup orange juice

2 tablespoons almond butter

$1\frac{1}{2}$ tablespoons apple cider vinegar

1 tablespoon extra virgin olive oil (optional)

$\frac{1}{4}$ teaspoon sea salt

Freshly ground black pepper to taste

OVER THE RAINBOW SALAD

When berry season is in full swing, I cannot get enough of this colorful salad. It's like having your main course and dessert all at once! Enjoy it with a bowl of vegetable soup for a truly satisfying experience.

1. In a large bowl, combine the salad greens, strawberries, blueberries, orange, onion, bell pepper, and pumpkin seeds.

2. In a small bowl, combine all of the dressing ingredients and mix well with a spoon until blended.

3. Pour the dressing over the salad, toss well, and serve.

HELPFUL TIP

Always be sure that your canned mandarin oranges have not been processed with sugar, which would acidify the recipe.

YIELD: 6 SERVINGS
· · · · · · · ·

5 cups grated cabbage (about 1 medium-sized head)

1 medium-sized carrot, grated

$\frac{1}{2}$ cup mayonnaise (soy, egg, and gluten-free) or Almond Mayo (page 78)

1 tablespoon apple cider vinegar

1 tablespoon prepared horseradish

1 tablespoon Sucanat sugar

$\frac{1}{2}$ teaspoon sea salt

COLESLAW

This simple slaw is tasty, crunchy, and so easy to prepare. The horseradish gives it a nice kick, while also alkalizing the dish.

1. In a large bowl, combine all of the ingredients and mix well with a spoon until blended.

2. Refrigerate for 30 minutes and serve.

BEET AND ORANGE SALAD

*This salad is not only delicious and alkalizing,
but also looks absolutely beautiful on the plate.*

1. Trim the ends of the beets. In a $4^1/_2$-quart saucepan, cover the beets with water and boil them for 30 minutes, or until fork-tender. Drain and let cool. Peel the beets and slice them into 1-inch rounds. Set aside.

2. Peel and remove the pith of the oranges. Separate the orange segments and slice them into $1/_4$-inch pieces. Set aside.

3. In a $1^1/_2$-quart saucepan, combine the orange juice, vinegar, orange zest, sugar, and salt over high heat. Boil the mixture until it reduces to about $1/_4$ cup. Remove from the heat and let cool.

4. In a large bowl, whisk together the cooled orange juice mixture and oil until emulsified.

5. Add the beets, oranges, and onion to the mixture and mix well with a spoon until combined. Refrigerate for at least 1 hour.

6. Arrange 1 cup of the salad greens in each of 4 individual salad bowls. Top each bowl with a portion of the beet-orange mixture and serve.

YIELD: 4 SERVINGS

• • • • • • •

4 medium-sized beets

2 large navel oranges

$1/_4$ cup orange juice

1 tablespoon apple cider vinegar

1 tablespoon orange zest

1 tablespoon Sucanat sugar

$3/_4$ teaspoon sea salt

$1/_2$ cup extra virgin olive oil

4 very thin slices red onion

4 cups mixed salad greens, torn into bite-sized pieces

HELPFUL TIP

If you are pressed for time, cook the beets one day in advance and keep them covered in the refrigerator. In a pinch, you could also use canned sliced beets and a can of mandarin oranges that have not been processed with sugar.

MARINATED ITALIAN VEGETABLES

YIELD: 8 SERVINGS

• • • • • • • • • •

4 cups cauliflower florets (about 1 head)

3 medium-sized carrots, diced

3 stalks celery, diced

19-ounce can mixed Italian beans or chickpeas, drained and rinsed

14-ounce can artichoke hearts, quartered

10-ounce can sliced mushrooms (optional)

$\frac{1}{2}$ cup diced jarred pimento or roasted red pepper

$\frac{1}{4}$ cup thinly sliced green olives (optional)

$\frac{1}{4}$ cup julienned sun-dried tomatoes

3 large cloves garlic, thinly sliced

$\frac{2}{3}$ cup extra virgin olive oil

$\frac{1}{4}$ cup apple cider vinegar

$\frac{1}{4}$ cup flaxseed oil

2 teaspoons dried basil

1 teaspoon sea salt

$\frac{1}{2}$ teaspoon dried oregano

Marinated vegetables keep well refrigerated and this recipe will go with almost anything as a side dish. I often add a couple of cups of this salad to cooked vegetable pasta shells and top with a small amount of grated Parmesan cheese as a quick lunch.

1. Fill half of a $4\frac{1}{2}$-quart saucepan with water and bring to a boil. Add the cauliflower, carrots, and celery to the boiling water. Reduce the heat to medium and cook for 15 minutes, or until the vegetables are slightly tender but not soft. Drain well and set aside.

2. In a large bowl, combine the chickpeas, artichokes, mushrooms, pimentos, olives, tomatoes, and garlic. Add the cooked vegetables to the bowl and toss well.

3. In a small bowl, whisk together the olive oil, vinegar, flaxseed oil, basil, salt, and oregano until emulsified. Pour over the vegetables and toss again. Marinate in the refrigerator for 1 hour before serving.

HELPFUL TIP

A bag of frozen cauliflower florets can be substituted for fresh cauliflower, making this recipe even easier.

ASIAN CHICKEN SALAD

This salad is a wonderful as a main dish. Packed with vegetables, it is alkalizing, highly nutritious, and very satisfying.

1. In a 10-inch skillet, toast the almonds over medium heat for 3 minutes, or until golden brown. Do not burn them. Set aside.

2. In a large bowl, combine the chicken, vegetables, and sesame seeds. Toss well.

3. In a medium-sized bowl, dissolve the miso in the warm water. Add the mayonnaise, ginger, tamari, sesame oil, sugar, salt, and pepper to the miso water and mix well with a spoon until blended. Pour over the salad and toss well. Top the salad with the almonds and serve.

YIELD: 8 SERVINGS

1/4 cup slivered almonds

3 cups cooked chicken breast, diced (about 12 ounces)

1 cup shredded Chinese or Savoy cabbage

1 cup snow peas, thinly sliced on the diagonal

1 large carrot, julienned or grated

1/2 cup finely diced celery

1/2 cup diced cucumber

1/2 cup diced green bell pepper

1/2 cup chopped scallion

1/2 cup chopped water chestnuts

1/4 cup raw sesame seeds

Dressing

1 tablespoon light-colored miso

1/4 cup warm water

1/2 cup mayonnaise (soy, egg, and gluten-free), or Almond Mayo (page 78)

3 tablespoons grated ginger root

2 tablespoons tamari

1 tablespoon sesame oil

2 teaspoons Sucanat sugar

Sea salt to taste

Freshly ground black pepper to taste

A History of Balance

The importance of balance has been slowly filtering down over the centuries from ancient civilizations to our modern society. The idea of a desirable middle between two extremes can be found in ancient Greek thought (the "Golden Mean"), Chinese philosophies such as Confucianism (the "Doctrine of the Mean") and Taoism ("yin and yang"), as well as the Indian religious tradition of Buddhism (the "Middle Way"). Borrowed from these belief systems, the concept also forms the basis of many of the Asian martial arts and Eastern medicine.

In recent years, the goal of equilibrium has begun to influence North American society in a number of ways, not the least of which is a growing awareness of pH balance. The attempt at balancing acidifying and alkalizing foods is no different than the objective of harmony put forth by great thinkers of the past. As it was then, moderation is still the true path to wisdom and good health.

WARM MUSHROOM AND ASPARAGUS SALAD

The citrusy taste of this salad lets you know that you are in for an alkalizing treat.

YIELD: 6 SERVINGS

$1/4$ cup fresh orange juice

2 tablespoons lemon juice

1 tablespoon lime juice

1 tablespoon orange zest

2 teaspoons lemon zest

2 teaspoons lime zest

2 tablespoons molasses

2 tablespoons rice syrup

2 tablespoons water

2 cloves garlic, pressed

2 teaspoons grainy mustard

12 ounces button mushrooms, halved

6 ounces asparagus, trimmed of tough ends and halved diagonally

1 red bell pepper, cut into thin strips

6 cups mixed baby salad greens

1. In a $4^{1}/_{2}$-quart saucepan, combine the fruit juices and zest over high heat and stir well. Add the molasses, rice syrup, water, garlic, and mustard. Stir well and bring to a boil. Immediately reduce the heat to medium-low.

2. Add the mushrooms to the saucepan and toss for 2 minutes. Remove from the heat.

3. In a 12-inch skillet, arrange the asparagus in a single layer. Add water to cover and bring to a boil over high heat. Cover, remove from the heat, and let sit for 1 minute. Drain the asparagus and place in a medium-sized bowl of ice water to prevent further cooking. Drain again.

4. Remove the mushrooms from the saucepan with a slotted spoon and reserve them in a medium-sized bowl.

5. Place the saucepan over high heat and bring the sauce to a boil again. Reduce the heat and simmer for 2 to 4 minutes, or until slightly thickened and syrupy. Remove from the heat and let cool slightly.

6. In a large bowl, combine the reserved mushrooms, reserved asparagus, red pepper, and salad greens. Toss well. Arrange equal portions in each of 6 individual salad bowls, drizzle with the sauce, and serve.

> **"The greatest wealth is health."**
> — Virgil, poet

ROBYN'S APPLE SALAD

This recipe was inspired by a salad that was made by the daughter of my good friends. It was so delicious that I had to convert it to an alkalizing version and include it here.

1. In a 10-inch skillet, toast the pumpkin seeds, stirring often, over medium heat for 3 minutes, or until they start to pop and turn slightly golden. Remove them from the skillet immediately.

2. In a large bowl, combine the salad greens, apples, onion, and toasted pumpkin seeds. Toss well.

3. In a small bowl, combine the apple juice, olive oil, syrup, butter, mustard, vinegar, salt, and pepper. Mix well with a spoon until blended.

4. Pour the dressing over the salad, toss well, and serve.

YIELD: 6 SERVINGS

$\frac{1}{4}$ cup shelled raw pumpkin seeds

6 cups mixed baby salad greens or chopped romaine lettuce

2 medium-sized apples, thinly sliced

$\frac{1}{2}$ cup thinly sliced red onion

Dressing

$\frac{1}{3}$ cup unsweetened apple juice

3 tablespoons extra virgin olive oil (optional)

3 tablespoons rice syrup

2 tablespoons almond butter

2 tablespoons grainy mustard

1 tablespoon apple cider vinegar

$\frac{1}{4}$ teaspoon sea salt

Freshly ground black pepper to taste

THAI SALAD ROLLS

These salad rolls are bursting with several tastes and textures. The pungent flavor of the cilantro combined with the aromatic basil and the crunchiness of the fresh vegetables makes this dish a winner.

1. Fill a 9-inch pie plate with warm water. Soak the rice paper wrappers in the water one at a time for about 5 seconds, or until soft. Shake off the excess water and transfer the wrapper to a flat surface.

2. Arrange a small amount of the bean sprouts and basil on the center of the wrapper. Add a portion of the carrots, bell peppers, and scallions. Sprinkle with some of the cilantro and sesame seeds. Do not overstuff the rolls or they will break.

3. Fold the sides of the wrapper over the filling. Fold the bottom of the wrap and roll it towards the top until completely closed. Lay the roll on a damp surface and place it in the refrigerator.

4. Repeat the process until all of the ingredients have been used. Serve with Asian Dipping Sauce.

YIELD: 16 ROLLS

16 rice paper wrappers

2 cups fresh bean sprouts, rinsed

1 cup coarsely chopped fresh basil (about 1$\frac{1}{2}$ ounces)

2 carrots, julienned

1 small red bell pepper, cut into thin strips

1 small green bell pepper, cut into thin strips

8 scallions, cut into thin strips

$\frac{1}{2}$ cup coarsely chopped fresh cilantro

2 teaspoons raw sesame seeds

1 recipe Asian Dipping Sauce (page 94)

BASMATI RICE SALAD

YIELD: 8 SERVINGS

• • • • • • • • • •

4 cups cooked basmati rice

$\frac{1}{2}$ cup minced fresh cilantro

$\frac{1}{2}$ cup dried currants

$\frac{1}{2}$ cup thinly sliced scallions

1 medium-sized green bell pepper, diced

1 medium-sized red bell pepper, diced

1 small English cucumber, quartered lengthwise and sliced into $\frac{1}{4}$-inch pieces

$\frac{1}{2}$ cup extra virgin olive oil

3 tablespoons fresh lemon juice

1 tablespoon ground coriander

2 teaspoons ground cumin

1 teaspoon ground cinnamon

Sea salt to taste

Freshly ground black pepper to taste

$\frac{1}{2}$ cup slivered almonds

When you're looking for something different in a salad, look no further than this delicious dish made with basmati rice and loads of vegetables. The combination of coriander, cumin, and cinnamon make it flavorful, alkalizing, and very healthy.

1. In a large bowl, combine the rice, cilantro, currants, scallions, bell peppers, and cucumber. Toss well.

2. In a small bowl, whisk together the oil, lemon juice, coriander, cumin, cinnamon, salt, and pepper until blended. Pour over the rice salad and toss well.

3. In a 10-inch skillet, toast the almonds over medium heat for 3 minutes, or until golden brown. Do not burn them. Top the salad with the almonds and serve.

"For both excessive and insufficient exercise destroy one's strength, and both eating and drinking too much or too little destroy health, whereas the right quantity produces, increases or preserves it. . . . This much then, is clear: in all our conduct it is the mean that is to be commended."

— Aristotle, philosopher

9. Sauces

Whether poured over savory dishes such as grilled fish and chicken, steamed vegetables, and pasta, or drizzled atop sweet treats such as pancakes, waffles, and cake, sauces are often the unsung hero of a meal. A good sauce can turn a decent main course into an unforgettable one. Unfortunately, a good sauce can also be highly acidifying. That's where this chapter comes in.

By making a few small changes to traditional recipes, including those for Hollandaise and béchamel, you can enjoy the flavor of a sauce without knocking your pH level out of balance. Swap out a few ingredients for less acidifying options, throw in a few alkalizing additions, and you can have a delicious pH-balanced complement to any meal.

YIELD: 1/2 CUP
• • • • • • • • •

1/2 teaspoon wasabi powder

2 teaspoons water

3 tablespoons rice syrup

3 tablespoons tamari

1 tablespoon apple cider
vinegar

1 tablespoon molasses

1 clove garlic, pressed

ASIAN DIPPING SAUCE

*This is a fantastic dip for egg rolls, spring rolls,
or rice paper vegetable rolls. Add some rice and stir-fried
veggies for a truly Asian-inspired meal.*

1. In a small bowl, combine the wasabi and water. Mix well with a spoon until blended.

2. Add all of the remaining ingredients to the wasabi water and mix well with a spoon until blended. Store any leftover sauce in the refrigerator for up to 2 days.

PUMPKIN SEED PESTO

*During the winter, I drive for two hours to get fresh basil just to
make this pesto. It goes well with pasta, baked potatoes, and cooked
vegetables. Mix it with a bit of mayo for a nice sandwich spread.*

YIELD: 1 1/2 CUPS
• • • • • • • • •

1 cup shelled raw
pumpkin seeds

3 cups lightly packed
fresh basil

3 large cloves garlic,
pressed

1/2 teaspoon sea salt

1/2 cup extra virgin
olive oil

1. In a 10-inch skillet, toast the pumpkin seeds over medium heat, stirring often, for 3 minutes, or until they start to pop and turn slightly golden. Remove them from the heat immediately.

2. In a food processor, combine the toasted pumpkin seeds, basil, garlic, and salt. Process until finely chopped.

3. Slowly add the oil to the processor, processing at low speed for about 30 seconds, or until blended. Be sure not to over-process, as you do not want the pesto to be soupy.

4. Refrigerate the pesto in a jar or airtight container for about 1 week, or freeze it in an ice cube tray, transfer the cubes to a heavy duty freezer bag, and keep in the freezer.

HELPFUL TIP

To keep the pesto looking fresh and green in the refrigerator, cover it with a thin layer of olive oil. When adding the pesto to a hot dish, stir it in at the last minute, as it can taste bitter when cooked.

HOLLANDAISE SAUCE

*This is an alkalized version of traditional Hollandaise Sauce.
I love to serve it on asparagus, cauliflower, and salmon.*

1. In a blender, combine the egg whites, salt, and cayenne pepper and process at high speed for 2 seconds.

2. In a 1-quart saucepan, heat the butter over low heat. Add the hot butter to the blender through the small opening in the cap, processing at high speed. Blend for about 30 seconds, or until thickened.

3. Add the lemon juice to the sauce and blend for a few more seconds. Transfer the sauce to a large glass bowl set in a pan of warm water to keep it warm before serving. Leftover sauce may be refrigerated in a tightly covered jar for 2 to 3 days and reheated by placing the jar in a bowl of hot water and stirring with a whisk.

> **YIELD: 1$\frac{3}{4}$ CUPS**
> • • • • • • • • •
> $\frac{1}{2}$ cup liquid egg whites, brought to room temperature
>
> $\frac{1}{4}$ teaspoon sea salt
>
> Pinch ground cayenne pepper
>
> 1 cup clarified butter
>
> 3 tablespoons fresh lemon juice, brought to room temperature

HELPFUL TIP

Instead of heating the butter in a saucepan, you can use a glass measuring cup with a spout and heat it in the microwave.

NON-DAIRY WHITE SAUCE

This is an alkalized version of your standard, run-of-the-mill white sauce. There is nothing fancy going on here, just great taste. Pour it on vegetables or into a casserole.

1. In a 1-quart saucepan, heat the butter over low heat. Whisk in the flour and cook, stirring often, for 1 to 2 minutes, or until thickened.

2. Add the salt to the saucepan, slowly whisk in the milk and cook, stirring slowly, for about 5 minutes, or until thickened. Store any leftover sauce in the refrigerator for up to 2 days, or in the freezer for up to 2 months, reheating it on the stovetop over low heat and blending gently with a whisk.

> **YIELD: 1$\frac{1}{2}$ CUPS**
> • • • • • • • •
> 2 tablespoons clarified butter
>
> 2 tablespoons light spelt flour
>
> $\frac{1}{4}$ teaspoon sea salt
>
> 1$\frac{1}{4}$ cups unsweetened almond milk

BÉCHAMEL SAUCE

Don't let the fancy name fool you. Béchamel is basically white sauce with a little pizzazz. This alkalized version can be used to make soups creamy, or ladled on top of veggies and meat.

YIELD: 1 ½ CUPS

• • • • • • • •

1 small onion

1 bay leaf

3 whole cloves

2 tablespoons clarified butter

2 tablespoons light spelt flour

¼ teaspoon sea salt

1 ¼ cups unsweetened almond milk

Pinch freshly grated nutmeg

1. Cut a small opening in the onion and place the bay leaf inside. Press the cloves into the onion and set aside.

2. In a 1-quart saucepan, heat the butter over low heat. Whisk in the flour and cook, stirring often, for 1 to 2 minutes, or until thickened.

3. Add the salt to the saucepan and slowly whisk in the milk.

4. Add the prepared onion and nutmeg to the sauce and cook, stirring occasionally, for 10 minutes. Discard the onion and cook, stirring occasionally, for 10 additional minutes, or until thickened. Store any leftover sauce in the refrigerator for up to 2 days, or in the freezer for up to 2 months, reheating it on the stovetop over low heat and blending gently with a whisk.

APPLE BUTTER SAUCE

This sauce is amazing on pancakes. So go have a look at the breakfast chapter and choose a pancake recipe already!

YIELD: 1 ½ CUPS

• • • • • • • •

1 cup organic apple butter

¼ cup water or unsweetened apple juice

¼ cup rice syrup

1 teaspoon ground cinnamon

1. In a 1-quart saucepan, combine all of the ingredients over low heat and mix well with a spoon for 5 minutes, or until blended and warm. If the sauce is too thick, add a little more water. Store any leftover sauce in the refrigerator for up to 2 days, or in the freezer for up to 2 months, reheating it on the stovetop over low heat and blending gently with a whisk.

CHEESE SAUCE

*Although cheese sauce is a favorite of so many people,
its acidifying ingredients pose a real problem to your pH balance.
This recipe cuts the acidity of this traditional sauce by using
clarified butter, almond milk, and a soft cheese.*

1. In a 1-quart saucepan, heat the butter over low heat. Whisk in the flour and cook, stirring often, for 1 to 2 minutes, or until thickened.

2. Add the salt to the saucepan, slowly whisk in the milk, and cook, stirring slowly, for 10 minutes, or until thickened.

3. Add the cheese and paprika to the sauce and stir until the cheese melts completely. Store any leftover sauce in the refrigerator for up to 2 days, or in the freezer for up to 2 months, reheating it on the stovetop over low heat and blending gently with a whisk.

YIELD: 2 CUPS

2 tablespoons clarified butter

2 tablespoons light spelt flour

$1/4$ teaspoon sea salt

$1 1/4$ cups unsweetened almond milk

$1/2$ cup grated curd cheese or mozzarella

$1/2$ teaspoon paprika

TOMATO BASIL CREAM SAUCE

I serve this sauce over steamed vegetables, pasta, and even grilled chicken. The fresh basil really makes it something special.

1. In a 1-quart saucepan, heat the butter over low heat. Whisk in the flour and cook, stirring often, for 1 to 2 minutes, or until thickened.

3. Add the salt to the saucepan, slowly whisk in the milk and cream. Cook, stirring slowly, for 10 minutes, or until thickened.

4. Add the tomato paste, garlic, and basil to the sauce and stir well until combined and heated through. Store any leftover sauce in the refrigerator for up to 2 days, or in the freezer for up to 2 months, reheating it on the stovetop over low heat and blending gently with a whisk.

YIELD: I CUP

2 tablespoons clarified butter

2 tablespoons light spelt flour

$1/4$ teaspoon sea salt

1 cup unsweetened almond milk

$1/4$ cup light cream

2 tablespoons tomato paste

1 clove garlic, pressed

3 tablespoons finely chopped fresh basil

ZESTY LEMON SAUCE

YIELD: 2 CUPS

• • • • • • • • •

2 tablespoons arrowroot powder

1 1/4 cups plus 2 tablespoons water, divided

Zest of 1 large lemon

3/4 cup rice syrup

Juice of 1 large lemon

2 tablespoons clarified butter

Pinch sea salt

Sweet and tangy, this sauce is simply delicious, especially when served warm over Gingerbread Cake (page 141).

1. In a small bowl, combine the arrowroot powder and 2 tablespoons of the water. Mix well with a spoon until blended and set aside.

2. In a 1-quart saucepan, bring the remaining 1 1/4 cups of water to a boil over high heat. Add the lemon zest, reduce the heat to medium-low, and simmer for 3 minutes.

3. Add the rice syrup to the saucepan and stir until dissolved. Add the arrowroot mixture and simmer, stirring constantly, for 5 minutes, or until thickened. Remove from the heat.

4. Add the lemon juice, butter, and salt to the sauce and stir until well combined. Store any leftover sauce in the refrigerator for up to 2 days, or in the freezer for up to 2 months, reheating it on the stovetop over low heat and blending gently with a whisk.

ORANGE GINGER SAUCE WITH TOASTED ALMONDS

YIELD: 1/2 CUP

• • • • • • • • •

1/4 cup almond slivers

2 tablespoons orange juice

1 tablespoon orange zest

1 tablespoon light olive oil

1 tablespoon rice syrup

1 tablespoon tamari

1 small clove garlic, pressed

1-inch ginger root, peeled and grated

1/4 teaspoon sea salt

This sauce is wonderful on stir-fried or steamed broccoli. The ginger root gives it a nice Asian flavor and is highly alkalizing.

1. In a 10-inch skillet, toast the almonds over medium heat, stirring occasionally, for 3 minutes, or until golden brown. Do not burn them.

2. In a small bowl, combine the toasted almonds with the remaining ingredients and stir well until blended. Store any leftover sauce in the refrigerator for up to 2 days.

ALMOND CREAM SAUCE

This simple sauce is not only excellent on grilled fish and poultry, it is also alkalizing, thanks to the almonds.

1. In a blender, combine all of the ingredients and process until smooth.

2. Transfer the mixture to a 1-quart saucepan and cook over low heat, stirring occasionally, for 5 to 7 minutes, or just until hot. Store any leftover sauce in the refrigerator for up to 2 days, or in the freezer for up to 2 months, reheating it on the stovetop over low heat and blending gently with a whisk.

VARIATION

For extra flavor, add a pinch of saffron.

YIELD: 3/4 CUP

. . . .

1/2 cup unsweetened almond milk

1/4 cup ground almonds

1 tablespoon chopped shallots

1/4 teaspoon sea salt

SAVORY LEMON SAUCE

The alkalizing effects of clarified butter, veggie broth, and lemon juice balance the mildly acidifying effects of spelt flour in this delicious sauce. Drizzle it over grilled fish or chicken for a lovely meal.

1. In a 1-quart saucepan, heat the butter over low heat. Whisk in the flour and cook, stirring often, for 1 to 2 minutes, or until thickened.

2. Slowly whisk the vegetable broth into the saucepan and cook, stirring often, for about 5 minutes, or until thickened.

3. Add the lemon juice and lemon zest to the sauce, stir until smooth and well combined. Store any leftover sauce in the refrigerator for up to 2 days, or in the freezer for up to 2 months, reheating it on the stovetop over low heat and blending gently with a whisk.

YIELD: 1 1/2 CUPS

. . . .

2 tablespoons clarified butter

2 tablespoons light spelt flour

1 cup yeast-free organic vegetable broth

Juice of 1 lemon

Zest of 1 lemon

BERRY SAUCE

Serve this deliciously fruity sauce over cake, pancakes,
or waffles for an extremely tasty treat.

YIELD: 2 CUPS

• • • • • • •

2 teaspoons arrowroot
powder

3 tablespoons water,
divided

2 cups unsweetened
frozen mixed berries

2 tablespoons Sucanat
sugar

1. In a small bowl, combine the arrowroot powder and 1 tablespoon of the water. Mix well with a spoon until blended and set aside.

2. In a 1-quart saucepan, combine the mixed berries and remaining 2 tablespoons of water. Bring to a boil over high heat, reduce the heat to medium-low, and simmer, stirring occasionally, for 5 minutes, or until the berries are heated through.

3. Add the arrowroot mixture and sugar to the berries. Reduce the heat to low and cook, stirring often, for 5 minutes, or until the sugar dissolves and the sauce thickens slightly. Store any leftover sauce in the refrigerator for up to 2 days, or in the freezer for up to 2 months, reheating it on the stovetop over low heat and blending gently with a wooden spoon.

HELPFUL TIP

If you want to remove the seeds from the berries, press the cooked berries through a fine mesh sieve with the back of a spoon before adding the arrowroot mixture and sugar. I like to keep the seeds in the sauce for their nutritional value and fiber content.

10. Vegetables and Grains

No matter how you look at it, eating more vegetables is the easiest way to alkalize your diet and achieve a pH-balanced body. But eating a giant plate of plain old steamed vegetables every day quickly becomes boring, and that boredom often leads to an indulgence in sweets and fast foods, tilting your system back towards acidity.

To avoid the boredom, here are a collection of amazingly flavorful recipes that feature lots of healthy and alkalizing vegetables, as well as a few hearty and satisfying grains. Once you familiarize yourself with these dishes, you will find it easy to mix and match other vegetables and grains, substituting one for another according to preference to create your own pH-friendly meals. The possibilities are endless.

MAHOGANY RICE

Originating in Japan, black japonica rice is a blend of short-grain black rice and medium-grain mahogany rice. Its nutty and mushroom-like flavor is perfectly complemented by the caramelized onions in this dish.

1. In a $2^1/_2$-quart saucepan, heat the butter over medium-low heat. Add the onions and cook, stirring often, for 25 minutes, or until dark brown and slightly caramelized.

2. Add the rice to the saucepan and cook, stirring often, for 2 minutes.

3. Slowly add the water and salt to the saucepan and bring to a boil over high heat, stirring once or twice. Cover, reduce the heat to low, and simmer, stirring occasionally, for 45 minutes, or until the rice completely absorbs the water. Check the tenderness of the rice occasionally, adding more water if necessary.

4. Remove from the heat and let sit, covered, for 10 minutes. Fluff with a fork and serve.

YIELD: 6 SERVINGS

3 tablespoons clarified butter

4 large onions, thinly sliced lengthwise

I cup black japonica rice or short-grain black and mahogany rice

2 cups water

$^1/_2$ teaspoon sea salt

WINTER SQUASH WITH AUTUMN STUFFING

The aroma of this dish is sure to bring everyone to the kitchen to see what's cooking. It is everything delicious about fall and winter. Serve on a bed of mixed baby salads greens for a well-rounded meal.

1. Preheat the oven to 375ºF.

2. Cut each squash in half lengthwise and scoop out the seeds. Arrange the halves face-down in two 9-x-13-inch baking dishes. Fill the dishes with $^1/_2$ inch of water and bake the squash for 40 minutes, or until tender, while you prepare the stuffing.

3. In a 12-inch skillet, heat the butter over medium heat. Add the onion and celery. Cook, stirring occasionally, for 5 minutes, or until tender.

YIELD: 6 SERVINGS

3 small acorn squash (about 3 pounds)

I tablespoon clarified butter

I small onion, finely chopped

I stalk celery, finely chopped

$1^1/_4$ cups all-pork sausage meat (about 6 ounces)

I small apple, unpeeled, cored, and finely chopped

$^1/_4$ cup raw pumpkin seeds

$^1/_4$ cup raisins

1/2 teaspoon ground cinnamon

Sea salt to taste

Freshly ground pepper to taste

$1^1/_2$ cups cooked brown rice, kasha, or millet

4. Add the sausage meat, apple, pumpkin seeds, and raisins to the skillet. Cook, stirring occasionally, for 5 to 7 minutes, or until the pork is cooked through. Add the cinnamon, salt, and pepper. Stir well.

5. Add the cooked rice to the skillet, stirring well to combine. Remove from the heat and set aside.

6. Once the squash are cooked, drain the baking dishes and turn the squash halves face-up. Spoon equal amounts of stuffing onto each half. Cover the pans with aluminum foil and bake for about 15 minutes, or until heated through.

ITALIAN-STYLE ROASTED VEGETABLE MEDLEY

Served as a side dish or tossed with pasta, these vegetables are simply delicious. Place them on a tortilla, add a dollop of Pumpkin Seed Pesto (page 94), top with some grated curd cheese or mozzarella, and wrap the whole thing up for a great lunch.

1. Preheat the oven to 400°F. Lightly coat two 9-x-13-inch baking dishes with vegetable oil and set aside.

2. In a large bowl, combine the garlic, onions, fennel, zucchini, eggplant, bell peppers, artichokes, and oil. Toss well.

3. Add the basil, oregano, salt, and fennel seeds to the vegetables and toss well.

4. Transfer the vegetables to the prepared baking sheets, spreading them out in a single layer.

5. Roast the vegetables for 35 minutes, or until lightly browned and fork-tender, and serve.

YIELD: 10 SERVINGS

6 large cloves garlic, coarsely chopped

2 large onions, sliced lengthwise

2 medium-sized fennel bulbs, sliced lengthwise

2 medium-sized zucchini, quartered lengthwise and chopped

I small eggplant, diced into 1-inch cubes

I large red bell pepper, diced

I large green bell pepper, diced

14-ounce can artichoke hearts, drained and quartered

$\frac{1}{4}$ cup light olive oil

I tablespoon dried basil

I teaspoon dried oregano

I teaspoon sea salt

$\frac{1}{2}$ teaspoon fennel seeds

ROASTED ROOT VEGETABLES

This dish is so versatile that I have actually eaten it for breakfast alongside cooked quinoa and a poached egg. It is a great addition to almost any meal.

YIELD: 8 SERVINGS

6 large cloves garlic, whole

5 medium-sized parsnips, diced into 1-inch cubes

4 medium-sized potatoes, unpeeled and diced into 1-inch cubes

2 large sweet potatoes, unpeeled and diced into 1-inch cubes

2 large onions, sliced lengthwise

1 medium-sized butternut squash, diced into 1-inch cubes

$^1/_4$ cup light olive oil

1 teaspoon sea salt

1. Preheat the oven to 400°F. Lightly coat two 9-x-13-inch baking dishes with vegetable oil and set aside.

2. In a large bowl, combine the garlic, parsnips, potatoes, onions, squash, and oil. Toss well.

3. Add the sea salt to the vegetables and toss again.

4. Transfer the vegetables to the prepared baking dishes, spreading them out in single layer.

5. Roast the vegetables for 35 minutes, or until lightly browned and fork-tender, and serve.

TURNIP PUFF

I must admit that I am a huge fan of this Turnip Puff. I could eat it for breakfast, lunch, and dinner. So don't let the turnip scare you! You may end up loving this puff as much as I do!

YIELD: 6 SERVINGS

6 cups diced turnips

$^1/_3$ cup egg substitute

2 tablespoons clarified butter

3 tablespoons light spelt flour

1 tablespoon Sucanat sugar

1 teaspoon baking powder

$^3/_4$ teaspoon sea salt

Pinch ground nutmeg

$^1/_2$ cup fine breadcrumbs from sprouted-grain or spelt bread

2 tablespoons melted clarified butter

1. Preheat the oven to 375°F. Lightly coat a $2^1/_2$-quart casserole dish with clarified butter or vegetable oil and set aside.

2. In a $2^1/_2$-quart saucepan, cover the turnips with water and bring to a boil over high heat. Reduce the heat to low, cover, and cook, stirring occasionally, for 10 minutes, or until fork-tender.

3. Drain and transfer the turnips to a medium-sized bowl or food processor. Mash or process well.

4. Add the egg substitute and butter to the turnips and mix well with a spoon or process until blended.

5. In a small bowl, whisk together the flour, sugar, baking powder, salt, and nutmeg. Add the dry ingredients to the turnip mixture and mix well with a spoon or process until blended. Pour the mixture into the prepared casserole dish.

6. In a small bowl, combine the breadcrumbs and melted butter. Mix well with a spoon to coat. Sprinkle the crumbs evenly on the turnip mixture.

7. Bake for 25 to 30 minutes, or until lightly browned on top, and serve.

INDIAN-STYLE ROASTED VEGETABLE MEDLEY

Vegetables roasted in this style are best served on a bed of basmati rice. Instead of using store-bought prepared curry powder, which can be acidifying, I combine turmeric with a few other spices to give this dish Indian flair.

1. Preheat the oven to 400°F. Lightly coat two 9-x-13-inch baking dishes with vegetable oil and set aside.

2. In a large bowl, combine the garlic, potatoes, onions, eggplant, cauliflower, and butter. Toss well.

3. Add the coriander, onion powder, turmeric, ground cumin, salt, cumin seed, and chili powder to the vegetables and toss well.

4. Transfer the vegetables to the prepared baking sheets, spreading them out in single layer.

5. Roast the vegetables for 35 minutes, or until lightly browned and fork-tender. Top with a handful of cilantro and serve.

YIELD: 10 SERVINGS

• • • • • • • • • •

6 large cloves garlic, coarsely chopped

4 medium-sized potatoes, unpeeled and diced into 1-inch cubes

2 large sweet potatoes, unpeeled and diced into 1-inch cubes

2 large onions, sliced lengthwise

1 medium-sized eggplant, diced into 1-inch cubes

1 medium-sized cauliflower, diced into 1-inch cubes

$\frac{1}{4}$ cup melted clarified butter

1 tablespoon ground coriander

2 teaspoons onion powder

1 teaspoon ground turmeric

1 teaspoon ground cumin

1 teaspoon sea salt

$\frac{1}{2}$ teaspoon black cumin seed (optional)

Chili powder to taste

Finely chopped fresh cilantro as a garnish

SPANISH-STYLE QUINOA

Instead of having rice with your Mexican feast, try this protein-packed alternative. Not only is it healthier than rice, it also cooks faster.

1. In a $4^1/_2$-quart saucepan, heat the butter over medium-high heat. Add the onion and bell pepper. Cook, stirring occasionally, for 5 minutes, or until the onion is translucent.

2. Add the garlic, paprika, and salt to the saucepan and cook, stirring occasionally, for 1 minute.

3. Add the quinoa to the saucepan and cook, stirring occasionally, for 3 minutes, or until lightly toasted.

3. Add the water to the saucepan and bring to a boil over high heat. Reduce the heat to medium-low and simmer, covered, for 15 minutes, or until the quinoa completely absorbs the water and appears translucent, and a ring appears on the seed.

4. Add the tomato, capers, and lemon zest to the saucepan and mix well with a spoon until blended. Cover, remove from the heat, and let sit for 10 minutes. Fluff gently with a fork and serve.

YIELD: 6 SERVINGS

2 tablespoons clarified butter

I medium-sized onion, finely chopped

I small green bell pepper, finely chopped

2 cloves garlic, pressed

I teaspoon Spanish paprika

$1/_2$ teaspoon sea salt

I cup quinoa

$1^1/_2$ cups water

I large tomato, seeded and finely chopped

I tablespoon capers, or $1/_4$ cup chopped green olives

2 teaspoons lemon zest

HELPFUL TIP

Always check the package of quinoa to see if the seeds have been rinsed. If they have not been rinsed, do so according to the directions on the package before cooking.

TWICE-BAKED SWEET POTATOES

*How can sweet potatoes taste so good and be so alkalizing,
you ask? I don't know, but our taste buds are very lucky
that both facts are true. This updated version
of baked potatoes is great as a side dish or as a snack.*

1. Preheat the oven to 400°F.

2. Pierce the potatoes a few times with a fork and arrange them on a 9-x-13-inch baking sheet. Bake for 1 hour, or until fork-tender. Remove from the oven and reduce the heat to 350°F.

3. Slice the potatoes lengthwise and carefully scoop the flesh into a medium-sized bowl, leaving $1/4$ inch of flesh on the skin. Set aside.

4. In a $1^1/_2$-quart saucepan, combine the butter, coriander, salt, and cinnamon over low heat and cook for 30 seconds, stirring once or twice.

5. Add the milk and cream cheese to the saucepan and mix well with a spoon until blended.

6. Add the milk mixture to the reserved potato flesh, fold in the scallions, and mix well with a spoon until combined.

7. Fill each potato skin with a portion of the mixture and transfer them to the baking sheet. Top the skins with paprika and bake for about 20 minutes, or until the filling begins to brown, and serve.

YIELD: 8 POTATO HALVES

· · · · · · · · · · ·

4 sweet potatoes, unpeeled

1 tablespoon clarified butter

1 teaspoon ground coriander

$1/2$ teaspoon sea salt

$1/4$ teaspoon ground cinnamon

$1/4$ cup unsweetened almond milk

$1/8$ cup cream cheese

4 scallions, finely chopped

$1/2$ teaspoon paprika

"Let the states of equilibrium and harmony exist in perfection, and a happy order will prevail throughout heaven and earth, and all things will be nourished and flourish."

— Confucius, philosopher

VEGETABLE CRUMBLE

The hearty mix of vegetables alone is reason enough to love this pH-balanced dish, but you will bend over backwards for another mouthful once you've tried it with the Crumble Topping.

1. Preheat the oven to 375°F. Lightly coat a $2^1/_2$-quart casserole dish with vegetable oil and set aside while you make the Crumble Topping.

2. To prepare the topping, combine the butter, flour, oats, and sesame seeds in a small bowl or food processor. Mix well with a spoon or process until crumbly and set aside.

3. In a $4^1/_2$-quart saucepan, cover the broccoli, cauliflower, squash, zucchini, bell pepper, and onion with water and bring to a boil over high heat. Reduce the heat to medium-low and cook uncovered, stirring occasionally, for 10 minutes, or until slightly tender. Drain the vegetables and transfer them to the prepared casserole dish.

4. Reduce the heat to low, add the butter and flour to the saucepan and cook, stirring often, for 2 minutes.

5. Slowly add the milk to the saucepan and cook, stirring constantly, until thickened.

6. Add the curd cheese, garlic, and salt to the saucepan and cook, stirring constantly, until blended. Pour the sauce over the vegetables.

7. Sprinkle the Crumble Topping over the vegetables and bake for 25 minutes, or until the topping is bubbly and golden brown, and serve.

YIELD: 8 SERVINGS

2 cups broccoli florets
(about 1 head)

2 cups cauliflower florets
(about $^1/_2$ head)

2 cups diced butternut squash

1 medium-sized zucchini,
coarsely chopped

1 small red bell pepper,
coarsely chopped

$^1/_2$ cup finely chopped red onion

2 tablespoons clarified butter

2 tablespoons light spelt flour

$1^1/_2$ cups unsweetened almond milk

$^1/_2$ cup finely chopped curd cheese
or mozzarella (about 4 ounces)

1 clove garlic, pressed

$^1/_2$ teaspoon sea salt

Crumble Topping

$^1/_4$ cup clarified butter

$^1/_4$ cup light spelt flour

$^1/_4$ cup old-fashioned rolled oats

2 tablespoons raw sesame seeds

**"Our bodies are our gardens—
our wills are our gardeners."**

—William Shakespeare

ASPARAGUS RISOTTO

A good risotto requires a little more concentration and tender loving care than most recipes, but you will thank yourself for dedicating the time and patience it takes to make this classic dish.

1. In a small bowl, combine the water and lemon juice. Stir well.

2. In a 12-inch skillet, arrange the asparagus in a single layer. Add the lemon water, cover, and bring to a boil over high heat. Remove from the heat and let sit for 1 minute.

3. Drain the asparagus, transferring the lemon water to a $4^1/_2$-quart saucepan. Transfer the asparagus to a medium-sized bowl and cover it with cold water to stop it from cooking. Drain and set aside.

4. In the $4^1/_2$-quart saucepan, add the vegetable broth to the lemon water and bring to a boil over high heat. Reduce the heat to medium-low, stir well, and let simmer.

5. In the 12-inch skillet, heat 2 tablespoons of the butter over medium heat. Add the onion and sauté for 5 minutes, or until translucent.

6. Add the rice to the skillet, stirring quickly for 2 minutes to coat the rice with the butter.

7. Add the simmering broth to the skillet $^1/_2$ cup at a time and cook, stirring constantly, for about 2 minutes each time, or until the rice completely absorbs the broth. Repeat this process for 20 minutes, or until the rice is tender and creamy but slightly firm. There may be broth left over.

8. Remove the skillet from the heat. Add the reserved asparagus, cheese, remaining tablespoon of butter, salt, and pepper to the rice and mix well with a spoon. Sprinkle with parsley and serve.

YIELD: 8 SERVINGS

• • • • • • • • • •

1 cup water

2 tablespoons fresh lemon juice

1 pound asparagus, trimmed of tough ends and chopped into 2-inch pieces (about 2 cups)

8 cups yeast-free organic vegetable broth

3 tablespoons clarified butter, divided

1 small onion, finely diced

$1^1/_2$ cups Arborio rice

$^1/_4$ cup grated Parmesan cheese

$^1/_4$ teaspoon sea salt

Freshly ground black pepper to taste

1 tablespoon chopped fresh parsley as a garnish

GREEK ROASTED POTATOES

Remember, potatoes are our alkaline friends. They are fat-free, cholesterol-free, and high in vitamin C and potassium. As potatoes are exposed to a particularly high amount of pesticides during normal production, buy organic whenever you can.

YIELD: 6 SERVINGS

6 large potatoes, peeled

$1/2$ cup extra virgin olive oil

2 cloves garlic, pressed

1 teaspoon dried oregano

1 teaspoon paprika

$1/2$ teaspoon sea salt

Freshly ground black pepper to taste

$1 1/2$ cups yeast-free organic vegetable broth

Juice of 1 lemon

1. Preheat the oven to 350°F. Slice the potatoes in half lengthwise and slice the halves into 2-inch pieces.

2. In a medium-sized bowl, combine the potatoes and oil. Toss well. Add the garlic, oregano, paprika, salt, and pepper. Toss well again.

3. Transfer the potatoes flat side down to an 11-x-17-inch roasting pan and set aside.

4. In a small bowl, combine the broth and lemon juice. Stir well. Carefully pour the liquid into the roasting pan at the corner until the liquid comes halfway up the sides of the potatoes.

5. Cover the roasting pan tightly with aluminum foil, place on the lowest rack in the oven, and bake for 45 minutes, or until the potatoes are fork-tender.

6. Discard the foil, increase the heat to 400°F, and bake for 10 minutes, or until the potatoes are crisped and slightly browned. Let sit for 5 to 10 minutes and serve.

> **"The greatest art is to attain a balance, a balance between all opposites, a balance between all polarities. Imbalance is the disease and balance is health. Imbalance is neurosis, and balance is well-being."**
>
> **– Osho, spiritual teacher**

SCALLOPED POTATOES

I barely had to do a thing to balance the pH of this traditional recipe. Makes you wonder if our grandmothers already knew about the importance of a pH-balanced lifestyle way back when.

1. Preheat the oven to 325°F. Lightly coat a $2^{1}/_{2}$-quart casserole dish with clarified butter and set aside.

2. In a $2^{1}/_{2}$-quart saucepan, heat 3 tablespoons of the butter over medium-low heat, whisk in the flour, sea salt, and pepper, and cook, stirring constantly, for 5 minutes, or until the mixture is smooth and bubbly.

3. Increase the heat to high and gradually whisk the milk into the saucepan $^{1}/_{2}$ cup at a time. Bring the mixture to a boil for 1 minute. Whisk in the liquid smoke.

4. Arrange a third of the potatoes over the bottom of the prepared casserole dish. Top with a third of the onions and a third of the sauce. Repeat the layers twice. Melt the remaining tablespoon of butter in the empty saucepan and pour it over the final layer.

5. Cover the casserole dish with aluminum foil and bake for 1 hour, or until the potatoes are fork-tender. Discard the foil and bake for 10 additional minutes, or until the potatoes are crisped and slightly browned. Let sit for 5 to 10 minutes and serve.

YIELD: 6 SERVINGS

4 tablespoons clarified butter, divided

3 tablespoons light spelt flour

1 teaspoon sea salt

$^{1}/_{4}$ teaspoon freshly ground black pepper

$2^{1}/_{2}$ cups unsweetened almond milk

$^{1}/_{8}$ teaspoon liquid smoke (optional)

6 medium-sized potatoes, peeled and thinly sliced

1 medium-sized onion, thinly sliced into rings

SWEET POTATO GNOCCHI IN SAGE BUTTER SAUCE

These gnocchi are worth much more than the time it takes to make them. And they are a delicious way to get nutritious and alkalizing sweet potatoes into your diet.

YIELD: 6 SERVINGS

• • • • • • • •

2 large sweet potatoes, peeled and cut into 1-inch chunks

2 cloves garlic, pressed

1 teaspoon sea salt

$1/2$ teaspoon ground nutmeg

2 cups light spelt flour

$1/4$ cup grated Parmesan cheese

Sage Butter Sauce

$1/2$ cup clarified butter

$1/2$ teaspoon ground sage, or 8 fresh sage leaves

$1/2$ teaspoon sea salt

Freshly ground black pepper to taste

1. In a $4^1/2$-quart saucepan, cover the potatoes with water and bring to a boil over high heat. Reduce the heat to medium and boil the potatoes for 15 minutes, or just until fork-tender. Do not overcook. Drain and press them through a potato ricer or food mill into a large bowl.

2. Add the garlic, salt, and nutmeg to the potatoes and mix well with a spoon. Add the flour and mix until the dough holds together but is still very soft and light. Use more or less flour as needed. Cover and refrigerate for 30 minutes.

3. Transfer the dough to a floured surface and divide it equally into 6 pieces. Using your hands, roll each piece into 1-inch thick tubes, sprinkling with flour if sticky. Cut the tubes into $1/2$-inch sections. Roll each piece over the prongs of a fork to give it ridges.

4. Fill three quarters of a $4^1/2$-quart saucepan with lightly sea-salted water and bring to a boil. Reduce the heat to medium. Add the gnocchi in batches of 10 to 12 pieces. Boil for 5 minutes, or until they float to the surface, then boil for 1 additional minute. Remove the gnocchi using a slotted spoon and transfer them to an 11-x-17-inch baking sheet lined with parchment paper or a large plate.

5. Let the gnocchi sit at room temperature for 30 minutes, or until firm, while you make the Sage Butter Sauce.

6. To prepare the sauce, heat the butter over medium heat in a 12-inch skillet until slightly brown. Immediately add the sage, being careful, as the butter may spatter.

7. Add enough gnocchi to cover the skillet in a single layer and sauté, tossing gently, for 5 minutes, or until heated through and slightly brown. Transfer the cooked gnocchi to a serving dish. Repeat the process in batches until all the gnocchi are done. Add the salt and pepper to the remaining sauce and stir well.

8. Pour the remaining sauce on the gnocchi, top with the cheese, and serve.

11. Main Dishes

This chapter presents a selection of North American meals as well as a number of dishes from around the world. The only difference between these recipes and their traditional versions is the ratio of vegetables to meat. Whereas meat most often plays the featured role in a main dish and vegetables the supporting part, here the roles are reversed.

A number of the following dishes are hearty and satisfying even though they include no meat. And in those dishes that include meat, I use an abundance of alkalizing vegetables and a very portion-controlled serving of animal protein. By using this guideline, your meals will become more alkaline, healthy, and so tasty. They'll also be a little easier on your budget, too.

YIELD: 6 SERVINGS
. . . .

$^1/_4$ cup light spelt flour

$^1/_2$ teaspoon sea salt

$^1/_2$ teaspoon paprika

3 whole bone-in skinless chicken breast halves (about 6 ounces each), quartered

3 tablespoons light olive oil, divided

2 medium-sized onions, coarsely chopped

14-ounce can artichoke hearts, drained and chopped

1 large red bell pepper, coarsely chopped

$^1/_4$ cup sliced green olives

2 large cloves garlic, pressed

1 teaspoon crushed dried rosemary

4 cups yeast-free organic vegetable broth

3 medium-sized carrots, chopped

8 ounces green beans, trimmed and chopped into 1-inch lengths (about 2 cups)

$^1/_4$ cup water

Juice of 1 medium-sized lemon

Freshly ground black pepper to taste

$^1/_4$ cup chopped fresh parsley as a garnish

Rosemary Lemon Dumplings

2 cups light spelt flour

1 tablespoon baking powder

$^1/_2$ teaspoon sea salt

$^7/_8$ cup unsweetened almond milk

2 teaspoons lemon zest

$^1/_2$ teaspoon crushed dried rosemary

MEDITERRANEAN CHICKEN STEW WITH ROSEMARY LEMON DUMPLINGS

Do not let the number of steps in this recipe scare you. This dish is quite easy to make and absolutely worth the time it takes to prepare.

1. In a plastic bag, combine the flour, salt, and paprika. Shake to mix. Add the chicken pieces to the bag a few pieces at a time, shaking to coat with the flour mixture. Knock off any excess flour from the chicken and reserve the leftover mixture.

2. In a $4^1/_2$-quart saucepan, heat 2 tablespoons of the oil over medium-low heat. Add the chicken and cook for 5 minutes on each side, or until slightly browned. Transfer the chicken to a plate and set aside.

3. Add the onions and remaining tablespoon of oil to the saucepan and cook, stirring occasionally, for 5 minutes, or until the onions are almost translucent.

4. Add the artichokes, bell pepper, olives, garlic, and rosemary to the saucepan and cook, stirring occasionally, for 5 minutes, or until the peppers are slightly tender.

5. Return the chicken to the saucepan and add the broth, carrots, and green beans. Reduce the heat to medium-low, cover, and let simmer while you make the Rosemary Lemon Dumplings.

6. Preheat the oven to 200°F. Lightly grease a 9-x-13-inch baking dish with clarified butter and set aside.

7. To make the dumplings, whisk together the flour, baking powder, and salt in a medium-sized bowl.

8. In a small bowl, combine the milk, lemon zest, and rosemary. Stir well.

9. Add the wet ingredients to the dry ingredients and mix well with a spoon until blended.

10. Drop tablespoonfuls of the dumpling mixture into the simmering stew. Increase the heat to medium, cover, and cook for 15 minutes, or until a toothpick inserted in a dumpling comes out clean.

11. Transfer the cooked dumplings to the prepared baking dish and place in the oven to keep warm.

12. In a small bowl, combine the reserved leftover flour mixture (from coating the chicken) and water. Mix well with a spoon until free of lumps and stir into the stew. Add the lemon juice and pepper to the stew and stir until heated through.

13. Divide the stew in 6 individual bowls, making sure to include 2 pieces of chicken per serving. Top with a few dumplings, garnish with parsley, and serve.

LINGUINI AND CLAM SAUCE

Lucky for us, clams are less acid-forming than other shell fish. So enjoy this pasta dish with that in mind, as well as a big salad.

1. In a 6-quart stockpot, cook the pasta for a few minutes less than directed on the package. Drain and set aside.

2. While the pasta is cooking, heat the butter over low heat in a 12-inch skillet. Add the oil and onion. Cook for 5 minutes, or until the onion is tender but not browned.

3. Add the garlic, 1 teaspoon of the salt, oregano, and chili flakes to the skillet and cook just until fragrant, being careful not to burn the garlic.

4. In a small bowl, combine the reserved clam liquid and flour. Mix well with a spoon until blended. Add the mixture to the skillet and cook, stirring occasionally, for 5 minutes, or until thickened.

5. Add the clams, light cream, and $1/4$ cup of the parsley to the skillet and continue to heat, but do not boil.

6. Add the pasta to the skillet and toss for 2 to 3 minutes, or until the pasta has absorbed the flavor of the sauce and is completely cooked.

7. Season with the pepper and remaining $1/2$ teaspoon of salt and pepper, top with the remaining $1/4$ cup of parsley, and serve.

YIELD: 6 SERVINGS
· · · · · ·

2 pounds spelt or brown rice linguini

2 tablespoons clarified butter

2 tablespoons extra virgin olive oil

1 large onion, finely chopped

4 large cloves garlic, pressed

$1 1/2$ teaspoons sea salt, divided

1 teaspoon dried oregano

$1/4$ teaspoon chili flakes

2 cans (5 ounces each) baby clams, drained, reserving liquid

2 tablespoons light spelt flour

$1/2$ cup light cream

$1/2$ cup chopped fresh parsley, divided

SUMMER PASTA

This recipe is a much more alkaline version of a similar but less nutritious dish I used to make. Served with mixed salad greens, this new and improved meal is perfect for both lunch and dinner.

YIELD: 4 SERVINGS

I cup boiling water

6 sun-dried tomato halves, chopped

10 ounces spelt or brown rice pasta

2 tablespoons clarified butter

14-ounce can artichoke hearts, drained and chopped

3 cups green and yellow zucchini, diced (about 3 medium-sized zucchini)

3 large cloves garlic, pressed

1 cup unsweetened almond milk

$1/4$ cup cream cheese

2 tablespoons fresh lemon juice

$1/4$ teaspoon liquid smoke

$1/4$ cup chopped fresh basil, or $1\frac{1}{2}$ tablespoons Pumpkin Seed Pesto (page 94)

Sea salt to taste

Freshly ground black pepper to taste

1. In a small heatproof bowl, combine the water and sun-dried tomatoes. Soak for 20 minutes, or until soft enough to cut easily. Drain and finely chop the tomatoes.

2. Cook the pasta according to package directions. Drain and set aside.

3. While the pasta is cooking, heat the butter over medium heat in a 10-inch skillet. Add the artichokes and sauté for 5 to 7 minutes, or until slightly crisp.

4. Add the sun-dried tomatoes, zucchini, and garlic to the skillet and cook, stirring occasionally, for 4 minutes, or until the zucchini is slightly tender. Transfer the vegetables to a large bowl.

5. Add the milk and cream cheese to the skillet and mix well with a spoon until blended.

6. Add the lemon juice and liquid smoke to the skillet and stir well. Pour the sauce over the vegetables. Add the cooked pasta, basil, salt, and pepper to the vegetables. Toss well and serve.

> "In all perfectly beautiful objects there is found the opposition of one part to another and a reciprocal balance."
> — John Ruskin, art critic

Moo Shu Pork

*I simplified this recipe by substituting rice paper wrappers
for the traditional Chinese flour pancakes.
The dish is now not only delicious, but also easy to make.*

1. Prepare the marinade by combining all of the marinade ingredients in a medium-sized bowl. Stir well. Add the pork to the marinade and mix well with a spoon until coated. Cover and let marinate in the refrigerator for 1 hour.

2. In a small bowl, combine the arrowroot powder and water. Mix well with a spoon until blended and set aside.

3. Fill a $4\frac{1}{2}$-quart saucepan with water and bring to a boil. Add the cabbage, celery, bell pepper, and carrot. Blanch for 3 minutes. Drain the vegetables and set aside.

4. In a 14-inch wok, heat the oil over high heat. Add the pork, scallions, and mushrooms. Stir fry for 3 to 4 minutes, or until the pork is fully cooked.

5. Add the blanched vegetables to the wok and stir fry for 3 additional minutes.

6. Add the arrowroot mixture to the wok and cook, stirring often, for 2 minutes, or until slightly thickened. Remove from the heat.

7. Fill a 9-inch pie plate with warm water. Soak the rice paper wrappers in the water one at a time for about 5 seconds, or until soft. Shake off the excess water and transfer the wrapper to a flat surface.

8. Place 3 tablespoons of the stir-fried pork and vegetables along the middle of the wrapper and roll up the wrapper like a crêpe. Transfer the roll to a serving dish that has been lightly coated with sesame oil. Repeat the process until no filling remains.

9. Top with scallions and serve.

YIELD: 6 SERVINGS

- - - - - - - - - -

12 ounces lean pork, sliced into $\frac{1}{4}$-inch strips

2 teaspoons arrowroot powder

1 tablespoon water

3 cups Savoy or Chinese cabbage, thinly sliced

3 stalks celery, thinly sliced into 4-inch strips

1 red bell pepper, thinly sliced

1 large carrot, cut into matchstick-sized pieces

2 tablespoons vegetable oil

8 scallions, thinly sliced into 1-inch strips

6 large button mushrooms, thinly sliced

6 rice paper wrappers

Finely chopped scallions as a garnish

Marinade

$\frac{1}{3}$ cup hoisin sauce

3 tablespoons tamari

1 tablespoon grated fresh ginger

1 tablespoon apple cider vinegar

2 large garlic cloves, pressed

$\frac{1}{8}$ teaspoon chili flakes

HELPFUL TIP

If you keep your pork in the freezer, try slicing it while still slightly frozen. This makes it easier to slice thinly.

FALAFEL BURGERS WITH TAHINI SPREAD

A tasty and quick light lunch or dinner, this dish is a great way to enjoy falafel and include a good selection of vegetables in your diet. Be sure to slice the tomato thinly, though, as it is mildly acidifying.

YIELD: 5 BURGERS

1 cup falafel mix, such as Casbah

$\frac{1}{2}$ cup shredded zucchini

$\frac{1}{2}$ cup cold water

$\frac{1}{2}$ cup plus 2 tablespoons light olive oil

5 sprouted-grain buns

1 large tomato, thinly sliced

1 small red onion, thinly sliced

1 large avocado, thinly sliced

Alfalfa sprouts

Tahini Spread

$\frac{1}{4}$ cup mayonnaise (soy, egg, and gluten-free) or Almond Mayo (page 78)

$\frac{1}{4}$ cup tahini

2 tablespoons fresh lemon juice

1. Line a 9-x-13-inch baking sheet with paper towel and set aside.

2. In a medium-sized bowl, combine the falafel mix, zucchini, and water. Mix well with a spoon until blended. Let sit for 10 minutes while you make the Tahini Spread.

3. To make the spread, combine the mayonnaise, tahini, and lemon juice in a small bowl. Mix well with a spoon until blended and set aside.

4. In an 8-inch skillet, heat 2 tablespoons of the oil over medium-low heat. Using your hands, shape $\frac{1}{4}$ cup of the falafel mixture into a burger-sized patty. Add the patty to the skillet, flattening it with a spatula. Cook for 3 to 4 minutes on each side, or until browned. Transfer to the prepared baking sheet and repeat the process until you have 5 burgers.

5. Place each falafel burger on a bun and dress with slices of tomato, onion, and avocado, and a few sprouts. Top with a tablespoon of the Tahini Spread and serve.

> "So divinely is the world organized that every one of us, in our place and time, is in balance with everything else."
> — Johann Wolfgang von Goethe, author

BAKED EGGPLANT ROLL-UPS

*If you've never had an eggplant roll-up, you are in for a novel treat.
Serve this dish with mixed salad greens tossed with Lemon
Poppy Seed Dressing (page 78) for a delightful dinner.*

1. Cut the eggplants lengthwise into six $1/4$-inch slices, discarding the shorter end pieces so that you have fairly uniform slices.

2. In a $4^1/_2$-quart saucepan, combine the water and salt. Bring to a boil over high heat, add the eggplant, and cook for 4 minutes, or until soft. Transfer to paper towels.

3. Preheat the oven to 350°F. Lightly coat a $2^1/_2$-quart casserole dish with vegetable oil and set aside.

4. In a 12-inch skillet, heat the oil over medium-low heat. Add the lamb, onions, potato, carrot, and garlic. Cook, stirring occasionally, for 10 minutes, or until the lamb is cooked through and the vegetables are tender. Drain off any extra fat.

5. Add the tomato sauce, nutmeg, and oregano to the skillet and stir to combine. Remove from the heat.

6. Arrange the slices of eggplant on a flat surface. Top each slice with a portion of the lamb mixture, a tablespoon of the feta cheese, and pepper to taste. Roll up each slice and place it in the prepared casserole dish seam-side down.

7. Pour the béchamel over the roll-ups, cover, and bake for 30 minutes. Uncover, bake for 10 additional minutes, or until lightly browned, and serve.

YIELD: 6 SERVINGS

• • • • • • •

2 eggplants

2 quarts water

2 teaspoons sea salt

1 tablespoon light olive oil

8 ounces ground lamb

2 medium-sized onions, finely chopped

1 large white potato, unpeeled and grated

1 large carrot, grated

3 cloves garlic, pressed

$1/2$ cup tomato sauce

$1/2$ teaspoon ground nutmeg

$1/2$ teaspoon dried oregano

6 tablespoons crumbled feta cheese

Freshly ground black pepper to taste

1 recipe Béchamel Sauce (page 96), or 28-ounce can chopped tomatoes, undrained

HELPFUL TIP

This dish can also be made in a layered style. Use 3 to 4 small eggplants sliced into $1/2$-inch rounds. Lightly sprinkle the rounds with sea salt and let them sit in a colander for 30 minutes to drain them of moisture. Rinse and pat dry. Layer the rounds and meat mixture, top with béchamel sauce or tomatoes, and bake as directed.

YIELD: 4 SERVINGS

I clove garlic, pressed

Juice of I lime

I tablespoon olive oil

$1/4$ teaspoon sea salt

4 boneless and skinless chicken breast halves (about 3 ounces each)

$1/2$ tablespoon vegetable oil

2 cups mixed salad greens

Mango Salsa

I mango, peeled and diced

$1/2$ cup finely chopped fresh cilantro

$1/2$ cup finely chopped English cucumber

$1/2$ cup finely chopped red and green bell pepper

$1/2$ cup diced tomato

$1/2$ cup finely chopped red onion

2 tablespoons seeded and minced jalapeño pepper

2 tablespoons rice syrup

Juice of I lime

I tablespoon light olive oil

2 teaspoons apple cider vinegar

$1/4$ teaspoon sea salt

GRILLED CHICKEN WITH MANGO SALSA

The lime juice, mango, and cilantro in this dish will make you feel as though you've traveled south of the border without ever leaving the comfort of your dining room.

1. In a medium-sized bowl, combine the garlic, lime juice, oil, and salt. Mix well with a spoon until blended.

2. Add the chicken to the bowl and toss well to coat. Cover and marinate in the refrigerator for 1 hour.

3. In a large bowl, combine all of the Mango Salsa ingredients, mixing well with a spoon until blended. Cover and refrigerate while you cook the chicken.

4. Remove the chicken from the marinade, discarding the marinade. In a 12-inch skillet, heat the vegetable oil over medium heat. Add the chicken and cook for 5 minutes on each side, or until cooked through.

5. Arrange $1/2$ cup of the salad greens on 4 individual serving plates, top with a piece of chicken and a portion of the salsa, and serve with a side of basmati rice.

> "What I dream of is an art of balance."
> — Henri Matisse, artist

SHEPHERD'S PIE

This dish is very comforting on a chilly day. Feel free to use any leftover mashed potatoes you have instead of making a new batch. They will taste just as great and save you some time.

1. In a $4^1/_2$-quart saucepan, cover the potatoes with water, bring to a boil over high medium-heat, and cook for 20 minutes, or until fork-tender. Remove from the heat and drain. Add the milk, butter, salt, and pepper to the potatoes and mash until well blended.

2. Return the saucepan to the heat and reduce the heat to low. Cook, stirring occasionally, while you cook the ground meat.

3. In a 5-quart sauté pan, heat the oil over medium-high heat. Add the ground meat, onion, and garlic. Cook, stirring occasionally, for 10 minutes, or until the meat is almost cooked through.

4. Add the mushrooms, carrots, corn, and green beans to the sauté pan and cook, stirring occasionally, for 5 to 7 minutes, or until the carrots are slightly tender and the meat is cooked through. Remove from the heat.

5. Preheat the oven to 350° F.

6. In a $1^1/_2$-quart saucepan, combine the broth, flour, and tamari over medium heat. Mix well with a spoon for 10 minutes, or until a thick gravy forms.

7. Lightly coat a 4-quart casserole dish with cooking spray and fill with the meat and vegetable mixture. Cover the top with the mashed potatoes and sprinkle with the paprika.

8. Bake uncovered for 30 to 35 minutes, or until lightly browned on top, and serve.

YIELD: 8 SERVINGS

3 large white potatoes, peeled and cut into 1-inch chunks

$^1/_3$ cup unsweetened almond milk

3 tablespoons clarified butter

$^1/_4$ teaspoon sea salt

Freshly ground black pepper to taste

1 tablespoon vegetable oil

12 ounces lean ground lamb, beef, or chicken

1 medium-sized onion, finely chopped

1 clove garlic, pressed

4-ounce can sliced mushrooms, drained

$^1/_2$ cup diced carrots

$^1/_2$ cup frozen corn

$^1/_2$ cup chopped frozen green beans

1 cup yeast-free organic vegetable broth

$^1/_4$ cup light spelt flour

2 tablespoons tamari

1 teaspoon paprika

YIELD: 6 SERVINGS

· · · · · · · · · · · ·

1 pound lean stew beef, cut into 1-inch cubes

1 teaspoon ground cumin

1 teaspoon ground cinnamon

1 teaspoon ground turmeric

1/2 cup light spelt flour

1 tablespoon light olive oil or clarified butter

4 cloves garlic, pressed

2 medium-sized onions, coarsely chopped

3 cups yeast-free organic vegetable broth

1 cup water

1/2 teaspoon sea salt

1/4 teaspoon freshly ground black pepper

1/4 teaspoon ground nutmeg

3 cups peeled and diced sweet potatoes (about 5 potatoes)

1/2 cup coarsely chopped dried apricots

1/2 cup dark raisins

1/4 cup thinly sliced orange peel strips (about 2 medium-sized oranges)

2 medium-sized carrots, coarsely chopped

Chopped fresh cilantro or fresh parsley for garnish

MOROCCAN BEEF AND SWEET POTATO STEW

A warm pot of stew is a wonderful thing on a rainy day. This recipe is quite hearty and will definitely hit the spot.

1. Preheat the oven to 350° F.

2. Sprinkle the cumin, cinnamon, and turmeric over the beef.

3. In a small bowl, combine the flour and beef and toss lightly. Shake off any excess flour from the beef and reserve it in a small bowl.

4. In a 4-quart ovenproof stockpot or Dutch oven, heat the oil over medium heat. Add the beef and cook, stirring occasionally, for 5 minutes, or until browned.

5. Reduce the heat to medium-low. Add the garlic and onions to the stockpot and cook, stirring occasionally, for 3 minutes, or until the onions are translucent.

6. Add the broth, water, salt, pepper, nutmeg, and reserved flour to the stockpot and cook, stirring occasionally, for 3 minutes.

7. Add the potatoes, apricots, raisins, orange peel, and carrots to the stockpot. Cover and transfer to the oven. Bake for 1 hour, stirring occasionally, or until the carrots and potatoes are fork-tender.

8. Garnish with cilantro and serve on a bed of basmati rice or quinoa.

FISH CAKES

Why buy frozen fish cakes when they are so easy to make at home? These are easy to prepare and better than anything you'll find in the supermarket freezer.

1. In a $4^1/_2$-quart saucepan, cover the potatoes with water, bring to a boil over high medium-heat, and cook for 20 minutes, or until fork-tender. Remove from the heat, drain the potatoes, and mash until well blended. Transfer the mashed potatoes to a large bowl to cool.

2. Add the salmon, onion, celery, parsley, salt, savory, and pepper to the potatoes and mix well with a spoon until blended.

3. Wet your hands with water to keep the patty mixture from sticking to your fingers. Using your hands, form the mixture into 8 patties. Transfer the patties to a large dish and refrigerate for 30 minutes.

4. Place the breadcrumbs, egg substitute, and flour separately into 3 small bowls. Lightly mix the egg substitute with a spoon for a few seconds.

5. In order, dredge each patty in the flour, egg substitute, and lastly the breadcrumbs. Return the patties to the dish.

6. In a 12-inch skillet, heat the butter and oil over medium-low heat, stirring once or twice to combine. Add 2 to 3 patties to the skillet and cook for 5 to 7 minutes on each side, or until golden brown. Repeat the process until all the patties are cooked and serve with a side of Coleslaw (page 86).

YIELD: 4 SERVINGS

• • • • • • • • • •

3 medium-sized white potatoes, peeled and quartered

4 ounces flaked cooked or canned salmon

1 small onion, grated

2 stalks celery, finely chopped

$1/_4$ cup chopped fresh parsley

$1/_2$ teaspoon sea salt

$1/_4$ teaspoon savory

$1/_4$ teaspoon freshly ground black pepper

1 cup finely ground sprouted-grain or spelt breadcrumbs

$1/_3$ cup egg substitute

$1/_3$ cup light spelt flour

1 tablespoon clarified butter

2 tablespoons light olive oil

> "Next to love, balance is the most important thing."
> — John Wooden, basketball coach

BROILED FISH WITH CILANTRO PESTO

This recipe goes very nicely with Indian-Style Roasted Vegetable Medley (page 105).

1. Set the oven to broil while you make the Cilantro Pesto.

2. To make the pesto, add the pumpkin seeds to an 8-inch skillet over medium-low heat. Toast, stirring often, for 3 minutes, or until golden brown. Remove from the heat immediately and transfer to a food processor.

3. Add the cilantro, parsley, water, oil, lime juice, garlic, salt, and chili powder to the processor and process until smooth. Add more water if too thick. Set aside.

4. Cut the fish into 4 equal portions and brush with the oil. Sprinkle it with the salt and transfer to a 9-x-13-inch baking sheet. Broil for 5 minutes on each side, or until the fish flakes easily.

5. Transfer the fish to 4 individual serving plates and top with a portion of the pesto. Garnish with a wedge of lime and serve with a side of cooked vegetables.

YIELD: 4 SERVINGS

8 ounces salmon, halibut, or tilapia

1 tablespoon extra virgin olive oil

1/4 teaspoon sea salt

4 wedges lime

Cilantro Pesto

1/2 cup shelled raw pumpkin seeds

1 cup fresh cilantro

1/2 cup chopped fresh parsley

1/4 cup of water

2 tablespoons extra virgin olive oil

2 tablespoons fresh lime juice

1 clove garlic, pressed

1/4 teaspoon sea salt

Pinch chili powder

Acid Rain: pH Balance in the Environment

Acid rain refers to precipitation that has been made acidic by chemical pollutants in the air, particularly sulfur dioxide emissions from coal-fired power plants and nitrogen oxide emissions from factory farming. While steps have been taken to reduce the amount of sulfur dioxide released from coal-powered electricity production, not much has yet been done about the nitrogen oxide problem caused by modern agriculture.

Unfortunately, the resultant acid rain acidifies lakes, streams, and marshes, poisoning numerous aquatic species and affecting the entire chain of wildlife based around them. In addition, it leaches nutrients and releases toxic minerals such as aluminum from the soil, thus making the foods we grow not only less nutritious but also harmful. Just as your body cannot thrive without a proper pH balance, neither can the planet. It is up to everyone to address these chemical imbalances in the environment.

MEATBALL CURRY

When I make meatballs, I tend to make lots of them.
Feel free to cut this recipe in half, or make the
whole recipe and freeze the leftovers.

1. In a small bowl, cover the nuts with warm water and soak for 1 hour. Drain and transfer to a food processor and process into a smooth paste. Add the onions, garlic, and ginger. Process until finely chopped and blended.

2. Add the coriander, cumin, paprika, salt, cinnamon, nutmeg, cardamom, turmeric, black pepper, cloves, and cayenne pepper to the food processor and process for a few seconds until blended.

3. Line two 9-x-13-inch baking sheets with waxed paper and set aside.

4. In a large bowl, combine the meat and one third of the processed onion mixture. Mix well with a spoon until blended.

5. Wet your hands with water to keep the meatball mixture from sticking to your fingers. Shape the meat mixture into $1^1/_2$-inch balls. Arrange 15 meatballs on each of the prepared baking sheets, leaving about 2 inches between each ball.

6. In a $4^1/_2$-quart saucepan, heat the clarified butter over medium-low heat. Add the remaining onion mixture and cook, stirring occasionally, for 3 to 5 minutes. Add the milk, water, and lime juice and stir until blended.

7. Gently add the meatballs to the saucepan. Cover and cook, without stirring, for 5 minutes. Reduce the heat to low and continue to cook, without stirring, for 30 minutes, or until the meatballs are cooked through.

8. Garnish with the cilantro and serve on a bed of basmati rice with a side of vegetables.

YIELD: 10 SERVINGS
(3 MEATBALLS EACH)
• • • • • • • • • •

1 cup unsalted cashew nuts

4 medium-sized onions, quartered

4 large cloves garlic, pressed

1 tablespoon grated ginger root

1 tablespoon ground coriander

2 teaspoons ground cumin

2 teaspoon paprika

1 teaspoon sea salt

1 teaspoon ground cinnamon

$1/_2$ teaspoon ground nutmeg

$1/_2$ teaspoon ground black cardamom

$1/_2$ teaspoon ground turmeric

$1/_2$ teaspoon freshly ground black pepper

$1/_4$ teaspoon ground cloves

$1/_4$ teaspoon cayenne pepper (optional)

2 pounds ground lamb or chicken

2 tablespoons clarified butter

14-ounce can coconut milk

1 cup of water

1 tablespoon fresh lime juice or fresh lemon juice

Chopped fresh cilantro as a garnish

STUFFED ZUCCHINI

*This vegetarian dish features delicious faux turkey
sausage and will have your meat-eating friends
coming back for seconds.*

YIELD: 4 SERVINGS

• • • • • • • • • • •

2 large or 4 small zucchini

2 teaspoons light olive oil

2 cloves garlic, pressed

2 vegetarian sausages, such as
Tofurky Italian sausages, finely
chopped

$1/_2$ onion, finely chopped

$1/_2$ red bell pepper, finely chopped

1 cup cooked basmati rice

1 teaspoon dried oregano

1 teaspoon dried basil

$1/_2$ teaspoon fennel seed

$1/_2$ cup crumbled feta cheese

$1/_4$ cup chopped shelled raw
pumpkin seeds

Sea salt to taste

Freshly ground black pepper
to taste

$1/_2$ cup tomato sauce or
spaghetti sauce

$1/_2$ cup vegetable broth

1. Preheat the oven to 375°F. Lightly coat a 9-x-13-inch roasting pan with cooking spray or olive oil and set aside.

2. Cut the ends off the zucchini and slice them in half lengthwise. Using a spoon, scoop out the flesh and seeds, leaving about $1/_2$ inch of flesh on the peel.

3. In a 10-inch skillet, heat the oil over medium-low heat. Add the garlic, sausages, onion, and pepper. Cook, stirring occasionally, for 5 minutes, or until the onion is translucent.

4. Transfer the sausage filling to a large bowl. Add the rice, oregano, basil, and fennel and mix well with a spoon until blended. Fold in the cheese until combined. Season with the salt and pepper.

5. Stuff the zucchini halves with the sausage filling, piling it as high as you can.

6. Transfer the stuffed zucchini to the prepared roasting pan, arranging them close together to keep them upright.

7. In a large measuring cup, combine the tomato sauce and broth. Mix well with a spoon until blended. Pour the mixture into the roasting pan, coating the bottom.

8. Cover the roasting pan tightly with aluminum foil and bake for 50 minutes. Discard the foil and bake for 10 to 15 additional minutes, or until the zucchini is tender but still slightly crisp, and the filling is slightly browned on top. Serve with mixed salad greens.

HELPFUL TIP

Save the flesh of the zucchini and add it to a vegetable soup.

VEGETABLE BEEF STIR-FRY WITH CASHEWS AND MANDARIN ORANGES

This spicy dish is light on meat but packed with vegetables. It is so yummy that no one will be asking, "Where's the beef?"

1. To prepare the stir-fry glaze, combine the water and arrowroot powder in a small bowl. Mix well with a spoon until blended. Whisk in the orange juice, tamari, sugar, ginger, garlic, and chili flakes. Set aside.

2. Chop the tops of the broccoli from the stalks and cut into small florets. Peel and finely slice the remaining stalks. Set aside.

3. In a 12-inch wok or skillet, combine the cashews and 1 tablespoon of the oil over medium-high heat. Stir-fry the cashews for about 1 to 2 minutes, or until lightly browned and toasted. Transfer the cashews to a small bowl and set aside.

4. Add the beef and remaining tablespoon of oil to the wok. Stir-fry the beef for 2 minutes, or until browned. Transfer the beef to a small bowl and set aside.

5. Add the vegetable broth to the wok and bring to a boil over high heat. Add the broccoli, snow peas, and red pepper. Stir-fry for 4 minutes, or until the broccoli is just tender.

6. Return the beef to the wok and stir in the glaze. Reduce the heat to medium and simmer for 2 minutes, or until thickened. Gently stir in the oranges.

7. Transfer to a serving platter and sprinkle with the cashews, scallions, and sesame seeds.

YIELD: 6 SERVINGS

• • • • • • • • • • •

2 medium-sized heads of broccoli

$\frac{1}{2}$ cup cashews

2 tablespoons vegetable oil, divided

12 ounces lean beef, cut into $\frac{1}{4}$-inch thick strips

$\frac{1}{2}$ cup yeast-free organic vegetable broth

1 cup snow peas, trimmed and spine removed (about 12 ounces)

1 red bell pepper, thinly sliced into 1-inch lengths

2 cans (11 ounces each) unsweetened mandarin orange slices, drained

8 scallions, finely chopped

1 teaspoon raw sesame seeds

Stir-Fry Glaze

1 tablespoon cool water

2 teaspoons arrowroot powder

$\frac{1}{3}$ cup orange juice

3 tablespoons tamari

1 tablespoon Sucanat sugar

2 teaspoons peeled and grated ginger root

2 large cloves garlic, pressed

$\frac{1}{8}$ teaspoon chili flakes

ITALIAN ARTICHOKE PIZZA

This is a much more alkaline version of pizza than your average pie, which is often made with acidifying refined wheat, meats, and cheeses. This pizza crust does have yeast, though. So if you have a yeast-related health issue, use the recipe for Rustic Focaccia Bread (page 45) instead.

YIELD: TWO 11-INCH PIZZAS

• • • • • • •

Crust

1 package active dry yeast

1 $\frac{1}{4}$ cup warm water

4 cups light spelt flour, divided

$\frac{1}{2}$ teaspoon sea salt

Italian Artichoke Toppings

1 tablespoon olive oil

2 cloves garlic, minced

2 cups artichoke hearts

$\frac{1}{2}$ teaspoon fennel seed

$\frac{1}{2}$ teaspoon dried oregano

$\frac{1}{2}$ teaspoon dried basil

1 $\frac{1}{2}$ cups tomato sauce

2 medium-sized zucchini, sliced

Grated curd or mozzarella cheese to taste

1. In a large bowl, sprinkle the yeast on the water and stir gently to dissolve.

2. Add 2 cups of the flour and the salt to the bowl and mix well with a spoon, or use a food processor, until a dough forms.

3. Add the remaining 2 cups of flour to the dough and mix well again until blended. Transfer the dough to a lightly floured surface.

4. Knead the dough for 10 minutes, or until smooth and elastic.

5. Lightly coat a medium-sized bowl with vegetable oil. Transfer the dough to the bowl and turn it over to coat. Cover and let rise in a warm place for about 30 minutes, or until it doubles in size.

6. Preheat the oven to 450°F and lightly coat two 12-inch pizza pans with vegetable oil. Set aside while you prepare the toppings.

7. To prepare the toppings, heat the oil over medium heat in an 8-inch skillet. Add the garlic and artichoke hearts. Cook for 3 minutes. Add the fennel, oregano, and basil. Cook, stirring often, for 2 minutes. Remove from the heat.

8. Lightly sprinkle a flat surface with flour. Poke the dough gently with your fingers to remove any air bubbles. Divide it in half. On the floured surface, roll and stretch each half into an 11-inch circle, leaving a ridge around the edge. Transfer the dough to the prepared pizza pans.

9. Spread $\frac{3}{4}$ cup of tomato sauce on each crust. Top both crusts with equal amounts of the zucchini, artichoke mixture, and cheese. Bake for 20 to 25 minutes, or until the toppings are lightly browned and the crusts are crispy. Let cool for 5 minutes and serve. For alternate toppings, see Other Clever Pizza Combos.

OTHER CLEVER PIZZA COMBOS

*There are endless combinations for alkaline pizza toppings.
And because they are so alkalizing you can add as many vegetables as you like.
Here are a few additional suggestions that feature enough ingredients
for two 11-inch pizza crusts.*

POTATO GARLIC PIZZA

In a small bowl, combine 6 minced cloves of garlic and 3 tablespoons of olive oil. Mix well with a spoon and spread equally on both crusts. Thinly slice 2 unpeeled potatoes and arrange the slices in a single layer on both crusts. In an 8-inch skillet, heat a tablespoon of olive oil over medium-low heat. Add 2 sliced onions and cook for 10 minutes, or until caramelized. Spread the onions equally on both crusts. Top with a little rosemary and grated curd or mozzarella cheese, and drizzle with oil. Bake according to directions.

BROCCOLI CLAM PIZZA

In a $4^{1}/_{2}$-quart saucepan, lightly steam 1 chopped head of broccoli and 2 diced red or yellow bell peppers for 10 minutes, or until tender. In a large bowl, combine the steamed vegetables, Non-Dairy White Sauce (page 95), a 5-ounce can of drained baby clams, 3 minced cloves of garlic, and $1/_2$ teaspoon of dried oregano. Mix well with a spoon until blended. Spread the sauce equally on both crusts and top with grated curd or mozzarella cheese. Bake according to directions.

SPINACH FETA PIZZA

In a 10-inch skillet, heat 1 tablespoon of olive oil over medium-low heat. Add 2 cups of baby spinach and 3 minced cloves of garlic and cook for 5 minutes, or until the spinach wilts. Spread the spinach equally on both crusts. Top with crumbled feta cheese and julienned sun-dried tomatoes, and sprinkle with dried oregano. Bake according to directions.

HELPFUL TIP

I stretch and press my dough out on a large piece of parchment paper then place it—paper and all—on a pizza stone that has been preheated in the oven. The shape of the pizza is more rustic and not perfectly round, but never sticks to the stone.

CHILI

YIELD: 10 SERVINGS
. . . .

2 tablespoons clarified butter

4 medium-sized onions, coarsely chopped

3 large green bell peppers,
coarsely chopped

I cup quartered button mushrooms

4 large cloves garlic, pressed

$1/4$ cup chili powder

I teaspoon ground cumin

I teaspoon ground cinnamon

I teaspoon sea salt

I teaspoon freshly ground black pepper

$1/8$ teaspoon ground cloves

$1/8$ teaspoon ground allspice

2 cans (28 ounces each) whole
peeled tomatoes, crushed into
chunks and undrained

2 cans (15 ounces each) kidney beans,
drained

2 cans (15 ounces each) black beans,
drained

2 tablespoons Sucanat sugar

I tablespoon apple cider vinegar

I teaspoon chipotle hot sauce

$1/4$ teaspoon liquid smoke

A cookbook would not be a cookbook without a proper chili recipe. There are so many flavorful facets to this chili that I sometimes ask my guests to guess all of its spices.

1. In a $4^1/_2$-quart saucepan, heat the butter over medium heat. Add the onions, bell peppers, and mushrooms. Cover and cook, stirring occasionally, for 5 to 7 minutes, or until the onions are translucent.

2. Add the garlic to the saucepan. Cover and cook for 1 minute.

3. Add the chili powder, cumin, cinnamon, salt, pepper, cloves, and allspice to the saucepan. Uncover and cook, stirring occasionally, for 2 to 3 minutes.

4. Add the tomatoes, beans, sugar, vinegar, hot sauce, and liquid smoke to the saucepan. Reduce the heat to low, cover partially, and cook, stirring often, for 30 minutes.

5. Remove from the heat and let sit for 15 minutes before serving.

12. Desserts

Although dense whole grain bread is much less acidifying than the average white loaf, whole grain flours do not usually make the best cakes or dessert loaves. To solve this problem, I generally use light spelt flour, which is a happy medium between pH-friendly unrefined whole grain flour and highly acidifying refined white flour. It does not produce the typical white cake or loaf, but still tastes wonderful and is the closest and least acidifying substitution for refined wheat flour that I have found.

Most important to remember, however, is that desserts— even the most alkaline versions— usually contain sugar and fat. That is why we are so fond of them. Although the ingredients in the following sweet treats are more alkaline than those found in traditional recipes, that doesn't mean you can forego self-discipline, which is perhaps the most essential ingredient for good health and a proper pH level. Always consider portion control, especially if you are trying to lose weight.

FRUIT TART WITH ALMOND CRUST

This is a beautiful dessert worthy of a special occasion. The effort it takes to make it will be rewarded with each bite.

1. Preheat the oven to 350°F. Lightly coat a 9-inch fluted tart pan (with a removable bottom, if possible) or a quiche pan with clarified butter and set aside.

2. If using ground almonds instead of almond flour, place them in a food processor and process for 1 minute, or until they are as finely ground as flour.

3. In a small bowl, whisk together the ground almonds, flour, sugar, and salt. Add the butter to the almond mixture and mix well with a spoon until combined. Spread the mixture in the prepared pan and press evenly against the bottom with your fingertips.

4. Bake for 10 minutes, or until the crust begins to brown, checking often after 8 minutes to avoid burning it. Transfer the pan to the refrigerator while you prepare the filling.

5. To prepare the filling, whisk together the flour and $1/2$ cup of the milk in a small bowl until fully blended and free of lumps. Set aside.

6. In a $1\frac{1}{2}$-quart saucepan, combine the remaining $1/2$ cup of milk, sugar, and salt over medium heat and mix well with a spoon until blended.

7. Add the flour mixture to the saucepan, mixing well with a spoon until blended. Cook, stirring constantly, for 5 minutes, or until thickened.

8. Add the lemon juice and lemon zest to the saucepan and cook, stirring constantly, for 1 additional minute. Remove from the heat and transfer to a glass bowl. Cover with waxed paper, pressing it gently against the filling to prevent a skin from forming. Refrigerate for 20 minutes, or until completely cool.

YIELD: ONE 9-INCH TART

Crust

$1\frac{1}{4}$ cups ground blanched almonds or almond flour

3 tablespoons light spelt flour

3 tablespoons Sucanat sugar

$1/4$ teaspoon sea salt

3 tablespoons melted clarified butter

Cream Filling

$1/4$ cup light spelt flour

1 cup unsweetened vanilla-flavored almond milk, divided

$1/4$ cup Sucanat sugar

Pinch of sea salt

2 tablespoons fresh lemon juice

2 teaspoons lemon zest

Fruit Topping

$1/2$ cup peeled and thinly sliced kiwis

$1/2$ cup fresh raspberries

$1/2$ cup fresh blackberries

$1/2$ cup fresh sliced strawberries

$1/2$ cup unsweetened canned mandarin orange slices, drained

Glaze

$1/4$ cup rice syrup

Juice of 1 lime

2 tablespoons water

1 tablespoon arrowroot powder

9. Spread the filling in the tart crust. Arrange your choice of fruit on the tart in concentric circles from largest to smallest. Try to cover all the pastry cream with fruit so that no filling shows through. Refrigerate while you prepare the Glaze.

10. In a 1$\frac{1}{2}$-quart saucepan, combine the rice syrup and lime juice over high heat. Bring to a boil, stirring often.

11. In a small bowl, combine the water and arrowroot powder. Mix well with a spoon until blended.

12. Add the arrowroot mixture to the saucepan and reduce the heat to medium. Cook, stirring constantly, for 5 minutes, or until slightly thickened. Remove from the heat and let cool for 5 minutes. Drizzle over the fruit.

13. Refrigerate the tart for at least 1 hour and serve.

APPLE OATMEAL CRISP

Nothing says home better than the aroma of an apple crisp baking in the oven. No one will be able to tell that this version is made with more alkaline ingredients and less fat than usual, and you will be happy to serve a healthy dessert to your family.

1. Preheat the oven to 375°F. Lightly coat an 8-x-8-inch baking dish with clarified butter and set aside.

2. In a large bowl, combine the apples, sugar, flour, cinnamon, and nutmeg. Mix well with a spoon until combined. Transfer the mixture to the prepared baking pan.

3. Pour the apple juice into baking dish at the corner, taking care not to rinse the flour and spices off of the apples. Set aside while you make the Oatmeal Topping.

4. To make the topping, whisk together the oats, flour, and sugar in a medium-sized bowl. Cut in the butter and mix well with a fork until crumbly.

5. Spread the topping over the apples and bake, pressing the topping into the apples with an ovenproof spatula occasionally, for 50 minutes, or until the apples are tender. Serve warm or at room temperature.

YIELD: 6 SERVINGS
· · · · · · · · · ·

4 cups peeled and thinly sliced apples (about 3 large apples)

2 tablespoons Sucanat sugar

2 tablespoons light spelt flour

1 tablespoon ground cinnamon

$\frac{1}{2}$ teaspoon ground nutmeg

$\frac{1}{2}$ cup unsweetened apple juice

Oatmeal Topping

1 cup old-fashioned rolled oats

$\frac{1}{2}$ cup light spelt flour

$\frac{1}{3}$ cup Sucanat sugar

$\frac{1}{4}$ cup chilled clarified butter

SLOW COOKER RICE PUDDING

YIELD: 8 SERVINGS
• • • • • • • •

4 cups scalded vanilla-
flavored unsweetened
almond milk

$1/4$ cup Sucanat sugar

$1/2$ cup Arborio rice

I cup dark raisins

I teaspoon ground cinnamon

This recipe works best in a small $3^1/2$-quart slow cooker. Whether you eat it for dessert or breakfast, rice pudding is one of the ultimate comfort foods.

1. Lightly coat a $3^1/2$-quart slow cooker with clarified butter and set aside.

2. In a $2^1/2$-quart saucepan over high heat, bring the milk nearly to a boil, stirring constantly. Remove from the heat.

3. Add the milk to the slow cooker and stir in the sugar until dissolved.

4. Add the rice to the slow cooker. Cover and cook on high for $1^1/2$ hours.

5. Add the raisins and cinnamon to the slow cooker and stir well. Cover and cook on low for 1 hour, or until the rice is tender and the pudding is creamy. Serve warm.

VERY BERRY COBBLER

YIELD: 6 SERVINGS
• • • • • • •

4 cups fresh or frozen mixed
berries (blackberries,
blueberries, and raspberries
are recommended)

3 tablespoons Sucanat sugar

2 tablespoons light spelt flour

Cobbler Topping

2 cups light spelt flour

$1/3$ cup Sucanat sugar

I tablespoon baking powder

$1/4$ teaspoon sea salt

$1/4$ cup chilled clarified butter

$1^1/4$ cups unsweetened
almond milk

Moist and bursting with flavor, this dessert is certain to satisfy anyone's sweet tooth. The berries cook to a delicious texture and are covered by a light and flaky topping. And yes, I have, on occasion, enjoyed this cobbler for breakfast.

1. Preheat the oven to 375°F. Lightly coat an 8-x-8-inch baking dish with clarified butter and set aside.

2. In a medium-sized bowl, combine the berries, sugar, and flour. Mix well with a spoon until combined.

3. Spread the berry mixture in the prepared baking dish and set aside while you make the Cobbler Topping.

4. To make the topping, whisk together the flour, sugar, baking powder, and salt in a medium-sized bowl. Cut in the butter, mixing well with a fork until crumbly.

5. Make a well in the center of the topping mixture and quickly stir in the milk, mixing just until moistened. The batter will be fairly thick.

6. Drop tablespoons of the batter on the berry mixture. There will be spaces between the mounds.

7. Bake for 35 to 40 minutes, or until the topping is golden brown. Allow the cobbler to cool for 10 minutes and serve.

STRAWBERRY SHORTCAKE

This shortcake reminds me of the delicious biscuits
that I used to enjoy at the shortcake socials of my childhood.
Better than anything you could get at a grocery store,
these little cakes are great with any type of berry.

1. Preheat the oven to 400°F. Lightly coat a 9-x-13-inch baking sheet with clarified butter and set aside.

2. In a large bowl, combine the strawberries and rice syrup, mixing well with a spoon until combined. Cover and refrigerate for at least 30 minutes.

3. In a medium-sized bowl, whisk together the flour, sugar, baking powder, and salt. Cut in the butter and mix well with a fork until crumbly.

4. Quickly stir the milk into the bowl, mixing well until a dough forms.

5. On a floured surface, roll or pat the dough into a 5-x-9-inch rectangle. Cut the dough equally into 12 squares and arrange them on the prepared baking sheet.

6. Bake for 12 to 15 minutes, or until the bottoms are golden brown. Let cool while you make the whipped cream.

7. Chill the cream in the freezer for 10 minutes. In a small bowl, combine the cream and stevia. Whisk thoroughly for 4 minutes, or until stiff peaks begin to form. Refrigerate until ready to use.

8. Split each cake square in half, as you would a biscuit, creating the bottom and top layer of each shortcake.

9. Arrange the bottom layers on 12 individual serving plates and pour $1/4$ cup of the strawberries and syrup mixture on top of each layer. Cover with the top layers and pour another $1/4$ cup of strawberries and syrup mixture on each shortcake. Top with 2 tablespoons of the whipped cream and serve.

YIELD: 12 SERVINGS

• • • • • • •

6 cups thinly sliced strawberries, divided

$1/3$ cup rice syrup

2 cups light spelt flour

3 tablespoons Sucanat sugar

1 tablespoon baking powder

Pinch sea salt

6 tablespoons chilled clarified butter

$2/3$ to $3/4$ cup unsweetened almond milk

Fresh Whipped Cream

1 cup whipping cream

$1/2$ teaspoon stevia

SWEET POTATO PIE

*Sweet potatoes are our ally in the world of food,
so add them to your menu whenever you get the chance—
even if it means enjoying them in a pie!*

YIELD: ONE 9-INCH PIE

• • • • • • •

2$\frac{1}{2}$ cups peeled and cubed
sweet potatoes
(about 4 medium-sized
sweet potatoes)

$\frac{1}{2}$ cup hot unsweetened
almond milk

$\frac{1}{4}$ cup Sucanat sugar

$\frac{1}{4}$ cup molasses

3 tablespoons clarified
butter

$\frac{1}{2}$ cup egg substitute

1$\frac{1}{2}$ teaspoon ground
cinnamon

$\frac{1}{2}$ teaspoon sea salt

$\frac{1}{4}$ teaspoon ground nutmeg

$\frac{1}{4}$ teaspoon ground ginger

$\frac{1}{4}$ teaspoon ground cloves

1 recipe Spelt Pie Crust
(page 138)

Fresh Whipped Cream

1 cup whipping cream

$\frac{1}{2}$ teaspoon stevia

1. In a 4$\frac{1}{2}$-quart saucepan, cover the sweet potatoes with water, bring to a boil over high heat, and cook for 20 minutes, or until fork-tender.

2. Transfer the potatoes to a large bowl or food processor and mash or process until smooth.

3. In another large bowl, combine the milk, sugar, molasses, and butter. Mix well with a spoon until blended.

4. Preheat the oven to 350°F. Lightly coat a 9-inch pie plate with clarified butter and set aside.

5. Add the mashed potatoes to the milk and beat by hand, or with an electric hand mixer, until soft and creamy.

6. Add the egg substitute, cinnamon, salt, nutmeg, ginger, and cloves to the potatoes and mix well with a spoon until blended.

7. On a floured surface, roll out the dough into a 9-inch circle and transfer to the prepared pie plate.

8. Pour the filling into the pie crust and bake for 40 to 45 minutes, or until the edges of the filling are set. Filling may still be slightly soft at the center, but will firm up as it cools. Check the crust periodically during baking. If it is browning too quickly, cover the edges with aluminum foil. While the pie is baking, make the whipped cream.

9. To make the whipped cream, chill the cream in the freezer for 10 minutes. In a small bowl, combine the cream and stevia. Whisk thoroughly for 4 minutes, or until stiff peaks begin to form. Refrigerate until ready to use.

10. Transfer the baked pie to a wire rack to cool for 10 minutes, then to the refrigerator for 30 minutes, or until completely cooled. Serve with the whipped cream.

Apple Pie with Currants and Almonds

*An apple pie dressed up with a few more alkalizing
ingredients is simply more of a good thing.
This unusual combination of ingredients works so well,
you may never make a plain apple pie again.*

1. In a 10-inch skillet, toast the almonds over medium heat, stirring often, for 3 minutes, or until golden brown. Do not burn them. Set aside.

2. In a small bowl, combine the currants and apple juice. Let the currants soak for 30 minutes. Drain off excess juice..

3. Preheat the oven to 425°F. Lightly coat a 9-inch pie plate with clarified butter and set aside.

4. In a large bowl, combine the apples, almonds, currant mixture, sugar, flour, lemon juice, lemon zest, cinnamon, and nutmeg. Mix well with a spoon until blended.

5. Divide the dough in half. On a floured surface, roll out one half into a 9-inch circle and transfer to the prepared pie plate.

6. Pour the filling into the pie crust and dot with pieces of the butter. Roll out the remaining half of the dough into a 9-inch circle and cover the filling. Seal the edges and cut 3 or 4 steam vents in the top.

7. Bake for 15 minutes, reduce the heat to 350°F, and bake for 40 to 50 additional minutes, or until golden brown. If the edges start to burn, cover loosely with aluminum foil and continue baking. Let cool for 10 minutes and serve.

YIELD: ONE 9-INCH PIE

$\frac{1}{2}$ cup slivered almonds

$\frac{1}{2}$ cup dried currants

2 tablespoons unsweetened apple juice

7 cups thinly sliced apples (about 5 large apples)

$\frac{1}{2}$ cup Sucanat sugar

3 tablespoons light spelt flour

1 tablespoon fresh lemon juice

1 teaspoon lemon zest

$\frac{1}{2}$ teaspoon ground cinnamon

$\frac{1}{4}$ teaspoon ground nutmeg

1 recipe Spelt Pie Crust (page 138)

2 tablespoons chilled clarified butter

SPELT PIE CRUST

This recipe is absolutely the closest you can get to a regular pie crust while still being only mildly acidifying. It is very adaptable to any recipe that requires a pie crust.

YIELD: TWO REGULAR 9-INCH CRUSTS OR ONE THICK 9-INCH CRUST
• • • • • • • •
2 cups light spelt flour

$\frac{1}{2}$ teaspoon sea salt

$\frac{1}{2}$ cup chilled clarified butter

7 to 8 tablespoons ice cold water

1. In a large bowl, whisk together the flour and salt. Cut in the butter and mix well with a fork or pastry cutter until crumbly.

2. Add the water to the mixture 1 tablespoon at a time, mixing well with a spoon until an elastic dough forms.

3. Divide the dough in half. Between 2 sheets of parchment or waxed paper, roll out each half into a 9-inch circle. For a thick crust, do not divide the dough before rolling it out into a 9-inch circle.

4. Use in your choice of pie recipe and bake according to the directions.

HELPFUL TIP

Cover the dough with plastic wrap and store it in the refrigerator for up to 5 days, or freeze it in a ball for up to 2 months, thawing it in the refrigerator when ready to use.

OATMEAL RAISIN COOKIES

This recipe actually makes a pretty darned healthy cookie. These snacks are great to put in kids' lunches.

YIELD: 36 COOKIES
• • • • • • • •
3 tablespoons water

1 tablespoon ground flaxseed

1 cup dark raisins

$\frac{1}{3}$ cup Sucanat sugar

$\frac{1}{4}$ cup rice syrup

3 tablespoon melted clarified butter

1$\frac{1}{4}$ cup old-fashioned rolled oats

$\frac{3}{4}$ cup light spelt flour

1$\frac{1}{2}$ teaspoon ground cinnamon

$\frac{1}{2}$ teaspoon baking soda

$\frac{1}{8}$ teaspoon sea salt

$\frac{1}{3}$ cup unsweetened flaked coconut

1. Preheat the oven to 375°F. Line two 9-x-13-inch baking sheets with parchment paper and set aside.

2. In a small bowl, combine the water and flaxseed. Stir well and let sit for 10 minutes.

3. In another small bowl, cover the raisins with hot water and let soak for 5 minutes. Drain off the excess water.

4. In a medium size bowl, combine the sugar, rice syrup, and butter Beat with an electric hand mixer on medium-high speed for about 30 seconds, or until well blended. The mixture should be grainy. Add the flaxseed mixture and beat for an additional 30 seconds, or until well blended. Set aside.

5. In a small bowl, whisk together the oats, flour, cinnamon, baking soda, and salt.

6. Add the dry ingredients, raisins, and coconut to the wet ingredients and mix well with a spoon until blended.

7. Drop heaping tablespoons of the dough on the prepared baking sheets, leaving about 2 inches between the drops of dough to allow for spreading. Bake for 8 minutes, or until puffy and slightly golden at the edges. The cookies will not look quite done, but do not overcook or they will not be chewy.

8. Remove the parchment paper liners from the baking sheets with the cookies still on them and set on wire racks to cool completely.

CHOCOLATE BROWNIES

These brownies are egg and dairy free, and so very moist and delicious. If you do not wish to add seeds or nuts, feel free to leave them out. The final product will still be amazingly tasty.

1. Preheat the oven to 350°F. Lightly coat an 8-x-8-inch baking pan with clarified butter, line the bottom with parchment paper, and set aside.

2. In a medium-sized bowl, whisk together the flour, sugar, cocoa powder, baking powder, and salt. Stir in the seeds and set aside.

3. In a small bowl, combine the water and milk, and stir well.

4. Add the butter and vinegar to the milk mixture. Mix well with a spoon until blended.

5. Add the wet ingredients to the dry ingredients and mix well with a spoon until blended.

6. Spoon the batter into the prepared baking pan, smooth it out evenly, and bake for 40 to 45 minutes, or until a toothpick inserted in the center of the cake comes out clean. Let cool for 5 minutes and serve warm, or refrigerate for at least 1 hour and serve cold.

YIELD: 8 LARGE BROWNIES

· · · · · · · · · ·

1 ½ cups light spelt flour

1 cup Sucanat sugar

¼ cup organic cocoa powder

1 teaspoon baking powder

½ teaspoon sea salt

½ cup chopped shelled raw pumpkin seeds, cashews, or macadamia nuts (or a combination)

½ cup water, brought to room temperature

½ cup unsweetened almond milk, brought to room temperature

⅓ cup melted clarified butter

1 teaspoon apple cider vinegar

CARROT PINEAPPLE CAKE WITH CREAM CHEESE FROSTING

This cake is full of flavor and texture. If Christmas morning were a food, this is what it would taste like.

YIELD: 9 SERVINGS

- ½ cup water
- 3 tablespoons finely ground flaxseed
- 2½ cups light spelt flour
- 1 cup unsweetened shredded coconut
- ⅔ cup Sucanat sugar
- 2 teaspoons baking powder
- 2 teaspoons ground cinnamon
- 1 teaspoon baking soda
- 1 teaspoon pumpkin pie spice
- ½ teaspoon sea salt
- 2 cups finely grated carrots (about 4 medium-sized carrots)
- ¾ cup canned crushed pineapple
- ¾ cup unsweetened vanilla-flavored almond milk
- ½ cup melted clarified butter
- ½ cup unsweetened applesauce
- ½ cup dark raisins
- ½ cup coarsely chopped shelled raw pumpkin seeds

Cream Cheese Frosting

- 8-ounce package light cream cheese, brought to room temperature
- ⅓ cup clarified butter, brought to room temperature
- ⅓ cup rice syrup
- 1 teaspoon stevia (2 packets)
- 2 teaspoons lemon zest

1. Preheat the oven to 350°F. Lightly coat a 9-x-9-inch baking pan with clarified butter, line the bottom with parchment paper, and set aside.

2. In a small bowl, combine the water and flaxseed. Stir well and let sit for 10 minutes.

3. In a medium-sized bowl, whisk together the flour, coconut, sugar, baking powder, cinnamon, baking soda, pumpkin pie spice, and salt. Set aside.

4. In a large bowl, combine the flaxseed mixture, carrots, pineapple, milk, butter, applesauce, raisins, and pumpkin seeds. Mix well with a spoon until blended.

5. Add the dry ingredients to the wet ingredients and mix well with a spoon until blended.

6. Spoon the batter into the prepared baking pan, smooth it out evenly, and bake for 40 to 45 minutes, or until a toothpick inserted in the center of the cake comes out clean. Prepare the Cream Cheese Frosting while the cake bakes.

7. To prepare the frosting, combine the cream cheese and butter in a medium-sized bowl. Mix well with an electric hand mixer for 3 minutes. Add the rice syrup and stevia, mixing for 2 additional minutes, or until fluffy. Stir in the lemon zest with a spoon.

8. Frost the cake in the pan after it has cooled in the refrigerator for at least 1 hour.

VARIATION

For a different taste, substitute parsnips for the carrots.

GINGERBREAD CAKE

I love this cake! It is pretty easy to prepare and makes the kitchen smell wonderful. I really have to watch my portion control with this one!

1. Preheat the oven to 350°F. Lightly coat a 9-x-9-inch baking pan with clarified butter and set aside.

2. In a large bowl, whisk together the flours, baking powder, ginger, cinnamon, nutmeg, salt, cloves, and allspice. Set aside.

3. In a medium-sized bowl, combine the milk, oil, molasses, sugar, ginger, and orange zest. Mix well with a spoon until well combined.

4. Add the dry ingredients to the wet ingredients and mix well with a spoon just until moistened.

5. Spoon the batter into the prepared baking pan, smooth it out evenly, and bake for 35 to 40 minutes, or until a toothpick inserted in the center of the cake comes out clean. Let cool for 5 minutes and serve warm with Zesty Lemon Sauce (page 98).

YIELD: 9 SERVINGS

$1\frac{1}{2}$ cups light spelt flour

$\frac{1}{2}$ cup kamut flour

1 tablespoon baking powder

1 teaspoon ground ginger

$\frac{1}{2}$ teaspoon ground cinnamon

$\frac{1}{2}$ teaspoon ground nutmeg

$\frac{1}{4}$ teaspoon sea salt

$\frac{1}{8}$ teaspoon ground cloves

$\frac{1}{8}$ teaspoon ground allspice

$\frac{2}{3}$ cup unsweetened almond milk

$\frac{1}{3}$ cup light olive oil

$\frac{1}{3}$ cup molasses

$\frac{1}{3}$ cup Sucanat sugar

$1\frac{1}{2}$ tablespoons grated ginger root

1 tablespoon orange zest

FRUIT SALAD

This is my favorite fruit salad combination, but you can make any combination you want. As long as your choice of fruit falls on the alkalizing side of the food list, you're good to go.

1. In a large bowl, combine all the fruit.

2. In a small bowl, combine the rice syrup and orange juice. Mix well with a spoon until blended, pour over the fruit, and toss well.

3. Sprinkle the fruit with the coconut flakes, refrigerate for 30 minutes, and serve.

YIELD: 8 SERVINGS

4 cups diced cantaloupe, honeydew melon, or watermelon

1 cup sliced strawberries

$\frac{1}{2}$ cup halved grapes or dark raisins

$\frac{1}{2}$ cup chopped pineapple

4 kiwis, peeled and sliced

1 1-ounce can mandarin orange slices, drained

2 bananas, sliced

$\frac{1}{4}$ cup rice syrup

$\frac{1}{4}$ cup orange juice

$\frac{1}{4}$ cup unsweetened flaked coconut

MOLASSES SPICE COOKIES

You just cannot beat these cookies. The gentle sweetness of the molasses
and the slightly spicy aftertaste is simply delightful any time of day.

YIELD: 24 COOKIES
• • • • • • • •
3 tablespoons water

I tablespoon ground flaxseed

2 cups light spelt flour

2 teaspoon baking soda

I teaspoon ground cinnamon

I teaspoon ground ginger

$\frac{1}{2}$ teaspoon ground cloves

$\frac{1}{8}$ teaspoon sea salt

$\frac{2}{3}$ cup Sucanat sugar

$\frac{1}{2}$ cup clarified butter

$\frac{1}{4}$ cup molasses

Sucanat sugar for coating

1. Preheat the oven to 375°F. Lightly coat two 9-x-13-inch baking sheets with clarified butter, or line them with parchment paper, and set aside.

2. In a small bowl, combine the water and flaxseed. Stir well and let sit for 10 minutes.

3. In a medium-sized bowl, whisk together the flour, baking soda, cinnamon, ginger, cloves, and salt. Set aside.

4. In a large mixing bowl, combine the flaxseed mixture, sugar, butter, and molasses. Mix well with a spoon until blended.

5. Add the dry ingredients to the wet ingredients and mix well with a spoon until blended.

6. Lightly coat a plate or pan with sugar. Using your hands, shape the dough into $1\frac{1}{2}$-inch balls and roll each ball over the sugared surface. Arrange the balls on the prepared baking sheets, leaving about 2 inches between the balls to allow for spreading.

7. Bake for 8 to 10 minutes, or until the edges are set but the middle of the cookie is still soft. Let cool for 10 minutes and serve.

RAISIN BUTTER TARTS

My mother used to make these wonderful treats when
I was a child. I would smell their delicious aroma
as soon as I walked in the door from school.

YIELD: 12 TARTS
• • • • • • • •
I cup dark raisins

I cup boiling water

$\frac{1}{4}$ cup shelled raw pumpkin seeds

$\frac{1}{2}$ cup rice syrup

$\frac{1}{4}$ cup Sucanat sugar

2 tablespoons clarified butter

$\frac{1}{3}$ cup egg substitute

I recipe Spelt Pie Crust
(page 138)

1. Preheat the oven to 400°F. Lightly coat 12 individual tart cups or a 12-cup muffin pan with clarified butter and set aside.

2. In a small bowl, combine the raisins and water. Let sit for 10 minutes.

3. In a food processor, grind the pumpkin seeds until they become a coarse meal. Set aside.

4. In a $2\frac{1}{2}$-quart saucepan, combine the rice syrup, sugar, and butter over low heat and cook, stirring often, for 3 minutes, or until warm and blended.

5. Drain the raisins and add them to the saucepan. Remove from the heat and let cool slightly.

6. Add the egg substitute and pumpkin seeds to the saucepan and mix well with a spoon until blended.

7. Divide the dough in half. On a floured surface, roll out half of the dough, leaving it $1/8$-inch thicker than you would for a pie. Cut the dough into circles that cover individual tart cups or halfway up the cups of a muffin pan. Transfer the circles to the prepared tart cups or muffin pan, pressing them in gently.

8. Spoon approximately 2 tablespoons of the raisin mixture into each tart and bake for 15 minutes, or until golden. Let cool for 15 minutes and serve. If using a muffin pan, cool the tarts in the pan for 10 minutes, gently remove them from the pan, and transfer them to a wire rack to cool completely.

LEMON LOAF

The more lemony the better, as far as alkaline eating goes.
This is a tangy and delicious way to get some lemons in your diet.

1. Preheat the oven to 350°F. Lightly coat a 9-x-5-inch loaf pan with clarified butter, line the bottom with parchment paper, and set aside.

2. In a small bowl, combine the water and flaxseed. Stir well and let sit for 10 minutes.

3. In a large bowl, whisk together the flour, baking powder, and salt. Make a well in center of the mixture and set aside.

4. In a medium-sized bowl, combine the flaxseed mixture, milk, sugar, butter, and lemon zest. Mix well with a spoon until blended.

5. Add the wet ingredients to the dry ingredients and mix well with a spoon just until moistened.

6. Spoon the batter into the prepared loaf pan, smooth it out evenly, and bake for 40 to 45 minutes, or until a toothpick inserted in the center of the cake comes out clean. Let cool on a wire rack while you make the glaze.

7. To make the glaze, combine the rice syrup, lemon juice, and lemon zest in a small bowl. Mix well with a spoon until blended.

8. Once the loaf has cooled completely, turn it out of the pan and transfer it to a large plate. Glaze the loaf with the rice syrup mixture and refrigerate for 30 minutes before serving.

YIELD: 1 LOAF

• • • • • • •

6 tablespoons water

2 tablespoons ground flaxseed

$1^3/4$ cups light spelt flour

2 teaspoons baking powder

$1/4$ teaspoon sea salt

$2/3$ cup unsweetened almond milk, brought to room temperature

$2/3$ cup Sucanat sugar

$1/4$ cup melted clarified butter

2 teaspoons lemon zest

Glaze

3 tablespoons rice syrup

1 tablespoon fresh lemon juice

1 teaspoon lemon zest

BANANA LOAF

This super yummy and remarkably low-fat recipe also makes great muffins. Just use a muffin pan instead of a loaf pan.

YIELD: 1 LOAF

• • • • • • • • •

6 tablespoons water

2 tablespoons ground flaxseed

1 cup mashed ripe bananas (about 3 bananas)

1 ½ cups unsweetened almond milk

½ cup Sucanat sugar

¼ cup unsweetened applesauce

¼ cup melted clarified butter

1 ¼ light spelt flour

½ cup teff flour

2 teaspoons baking powder

1 teaspoon baking soda

1. Preheat the oven to 350°F. Lightly coat a 9-x-5-inch loaf pan with clarified butter, line the bottom with parchment paper, and set aside.

2. In a small bowl, combine the water and flaxseed. Stir well and let sit for 10 minutes.

3. In a large bowl, combine the flaxseed mixture, bananas, milk, sugar, applesauce, and butter. Mix well with a spoon until blended. Set aside.

4. In a small bowl, whisk together the flours, baking powder, and baking soda.

5. Add the dry ingredients to the wet ingredients and mix well with a spoon just until moistened.

6. Spoon the batter into the prepared loaf pan, smooth it out evenly, and bake for 75 minutes, or until a toothpick inserted in the center of the loaf comes out clean. Let cool for 15 minutes before removing the bread from the pan.

VARIATION

To make muffins instead, preheat the oven to 350°F and lightly coat a 12-cup muffin pan. Prepare the batter according to the recipe and spoon it into the muffin cups, filling them a little over halfway. Bake for 20 to 25 minutes, or until a toothpick inserted in the center of a muffin comes out clean. Cool for 15 minutes and serve.

Metric Conversion Tables

COMMON LIQUID CONVERSIONS

Measurement	=	Milliliters
1/4 teaspoon	=	1.25 milliliters
1/2 teaspoon	=	2.50 milliliters
3/4 teaspoon	=	3.75 milliliters
1 teaspoon	=	5.00 milliliters
1 1/4 teaspoons	=	6.25 milliliters
1 1/2 teaspoons	=	7.50 milliliters
1 3/4 teaspoons	=	8.75 milliliters
2 teaspoons	=	10.0 milliliters
1 tablespoon	=	15.0 milliliters
2 tablespoons	=	30.0 milliliters

Measurement	=	Liters
1/4 cup	=	0.06 liters
1/2 cup	=	0.12 liters
3/4 cup	=	0.18 liters
1 cup	=	0.24 liters
1 1/4 cups	=	0.30 liters
1 1/2 cups	=	0.36 liters
2 cups	=	0.48 liters
2 1/2 cups	=	0.60 liters
3 cups	=	0.72 liters
3 1/2 cups	=	0.84 liters
4 cups	=	0.96 liters
4 1/2 cups	=	1.08 liters
5 cups	=	1.20 liters
5 1/2 cups	=	1.32 liters

CONVERTING FAHRENHEIT TO CELSIUS

Fahrenheit	=	Celsius
200–205	=	95
220–225	=	105
245–250	=	120
275	=	135
300–305	=	150
325–330	=	165
345–350	=	175
370–375	=	190
400–405	=	205
425–430	=	220
445–450	=	230
470–475	=	245
500	=	260

CONVERSION FORMULAS

LIQUID		
When You Know	Multiply By	To Determine
teaspoons	5.0	milliliters
tablespoons	15.0	milliliters
fluid ounces	30.0	milliliters
cups	0.24	liters
pints	0.47	liters
quarts	0.95	liters

WEIGHT		
When You Know	Multiply By	To Determine
ounces	28.0	grams
pounds	0.45	kilograms

Appendix

International Menus

Following a pH-balanced diet doesn't mean that you can't experience all of the flavors and textures found in the many different cuisines from around the world. Have a spicy Mexican night or a fabulous Italian meal, and still be confident that you are eating in a healthful and pH-balanced way. Below are a few internationally inspired meals that can be created by combining recipes in this book.

American Harvest Menu

Pumpkin Ginger Pear Soup (page 69)

Herbed Spelt Biscuits (page 48)

Winter Squash with Autumn Stuffing (page 102)

Apple Oatmeal Crisp (page 133)

Greek Menu

Warm Artichoke Dip (page 57) with vegetable crudités

Greek Roasted Potatoes (page 110)

Baked Eggplant Roll-Ups (page 119)

Raisin Butter Tarts (page 142)

Asian Menu

Miso Soup (page 68)

Moo Shu Pork (page 117) with Asian Dipping Sauce (page 94)

Mahogany Rice (page 102)

Fruit Salad (page 141)

Indian Menu

Indian Lentil Soup (page 75)

Indian-Style Roasted Vegetable Medley (page 105)

Meatball Curry (page 125) with basmati rice

Coconut Macaroons (page 64)

Italian Menu #1

Roasted Garlic Soup (page 67)

Marinated Italian Vegetables (page 88)

Spelt Pasta with Tomato Basil
Cream Sauce (page 97)

Fruit Tart with Almond Crust (page 132)

Italian Menu #2

Rustic Focaccia Bread (page 45)

Fennel and Orange Salad (page 84)

Summer Pasta (page 116)

Lemon Bars (page 64)

Mediterranean Menu

Creamy Kale and Lentil Soup (page 66)

Shrimp-Stuffed Avocado Salad (page 85)

Stuffed Zucchini (page 126)

Apple Pie with Currents and Almonds (page 137)

Mexican Menu

Chunky Black Bean Dip (page 58) with Spelt
Tortilla Crisps (page 61)

Broiled Fish with Cilantro Pesto (page 124)

Spanish-Style Quinoa (page 106)

Lemon Loaf (page 143)

Middle Eastern Menu #1

Baba Ganoush (page 60)
with Kamut Flat Bread (page 46)

Quinoa Tabouli Salad (page 83)

Mediterranean Chicken Stew with Rosemary
Lemon Dumplings (page 114)

Fruit Salad (page 141)

Middle Eastern Menu #2

Quinoa Tabouli Salad (page 83)

Falafel Burgers with Tahini Spread (page 118)

Slow Cooker Rice Pudding (page 134)

Thai Menu

Thai Salad Rolls (page 91)
with Asian Dipping Sauce (page 94)

Mahogany Rice (page 102)

Grilled Chicken with Mango Salsa
(page 120)

Fruit Salad (page 141)

United Kingdom Menu

Leek and Potato Soup (page 72)

Shepherd's Pie (page 121)

Very Berry Cobbler (page 134)

Resources

Now that you have decided to change your life through pH-balanced eating, you may be wondering where to find some of the less common ingredients mentioned in this book. If you cannot buy a particular recipe item at your local market, here are a few resources to help you locate a store near you that carries it. Many of the following companies even take online orders.

Amazing Grass Organic Green SuperFoods
PO Box 475576
San Francisco, CA 94147
866-472-7711
info@amazinggrass.com
www.amazinggrass.com
Amazing Grass Green SuperFood is a powdered nutritional supplement. It is a healthy blend of fruits, vegetables, herbs, and other greens that can boost your immune system and alkalize your system. Amazing Grass Green SuperFood is certified organic.

The Center for Better Bones
605 Franklin Park Drive
East Syracuse, NY 13057
315-437-9384
888-206-7119
info@betterbones.com
www.betterbones.com

Founded by Dr. Susan E. Brown, the Center for Better Bones offers a comprehensive, whole-body approach to bone health. It supports healthy bone growth and regeneration through nutrition and lifestyle choices that include balancing your pH level. In addition to books, DVDs, and CDs, the website features pH test strips and complete pH test kits for purchase.

Blue Diamond Almonds
800-987-2329
customerservice@bdgrowers.com
www.bluediamond.com
Blue Diamond Almonds makes Almond Breeze almond milk and many other almond products, such as almond butter.

Bob's Red Mill Natural Foods
13521 SE Pheasant Court
Milwaukie, OR 97222

www.bobsredmill.com
800-349-2173
800-553-2258
Bob's Red Mill Natural Foods produces a wide variety of whole grain products, including arrowroot, amaranth, and gluten-free flours.

Encore Woodland
www.tasteofwoodland.com
Encore Woodland produces Hickory Liquid Smoke Flavor.

Feel Good Natural Health Stores
129 King St. East
Oshawa, ON L1H 1C2
Canada
905-571-1100
877-677-7797
www.feelgoodnatural.com
This company features the GREENS Plus line of supplements, not to mention protein powders and pH-testing paper. They also ship internationally.

Follow Your Heart®
PO Box 9400
Canoga Park, CA 91309
818-725-2820
fyhinfo@followyourheart.com
www.followyourheart.com
Follow Your Heart® makes an eggless mayonnaise called Vegenaise as well as a variety of other vegetarian products.

Food for Life
800-797-5090
951-279-5090
www.foodforlife.com
Food for Life offers sprouted-grain breads and over sixty other bread products, including several yeast-free options.

Lundberg Family Farms
5370 Church Street
PO Box 369
Richvale, CA 95974
530-882-4551
info@lundberg.com
www.lundberg.com
Lundberg Family Farms makes high quality brown rice syrup.

Orange Peel Enterprises, Inc.
2183 Ponce De Leon Cir.
Vero Beach, FL 32960
800-643-1210
info@greensplus.com
www.greensplus.com
This website features the GREENS Plus line of supplements, including an alkalizing greens powder called greens+.

Verve Naturals
7018 Wellington Rd., 124 S
Guelph, ON N1H 6J4
Canada
info@puresource.ca
www.puresource.ca
888-313-3369
Verve Naturals makes Verve Margarine, which is made from flax oil and is a good source of omega-3 fatty acids.

Wholesome Sweeteners
8016 Highway 90-A
Sugar Land, TX 77478
800-680-1896
cs@organicsugars.biz
www.wholesomesweeteners.com
Wholesome Sweeteners produces a variety of alternative sweeteners, including their trademarked Sucanat Organic Sugar.

Index

OTHER SQUAREONE TITLES OF INTEREST

THE ACID-ALKALINE FOOD GUIDE
SECOND EDITION
A Quick Reference to Foods & Their Effect on pH Levels

Dr. Susan E. Brown and Larry Trivieri, Jr.

In the last few years, researchers around the world have reported the importance of acid-alkaline balance. When the body enjoys pH balance, you experience radiant good health. When the body is not in balance, the disease process begins, resulting in problems ranging from bone loss to premature aging and more. The key to a healthy pH is proper diet, but for a long time, acid-alkaline food guides have included only a small number of foods. Or they did, until now.

The Acid-Alkaline Food Guide is a complete resource for people who want to widen their food choices. The book begins by explaining how the acid-alkaline environment of the body is influenced by foods. It then presents a list of thousands of foods and their acid-alkaline effects. Included are not only single foods, such as fruits and vegetables, but also popular combination and even fast foods, like burgers and fries. In each case, you'll not only discover whether a food is acidifying or alkalizing, but you'll learn the *degree* to which that food affects the body. Informative insets guide you in choosing the food that's right for you.

The first book of its kind, *The Acid-Alkaline Food Guide* will quickly become the resource you turn to at home, in restaurants, and whenever you want to select a food that can help you reach your health and dietary goals.

$8.95 • 224 pages • 4 x 7-inch mass paperback • ISBN 978-0-7570-0393-6

THE ACID-ALKALINE LIFESTYLE

The Complete Program for Better Health and Vitality

Larry Trivieri, Jr. and Neil Raff, MD

The human body is a truly magnificent creation. And because of its ability to regulate, balance, repair, and protect itself, the latest scientific research shows that each of us has the capacity to function well for at least one hundred and twenty years. So why do most of us make it only into our seventies? Why are so many of us afflicted with degenerative diseases? And why are the disorders that once plagued only the elderly—heart disease, diabetes, osteoporosis, arthritis, and cancer—now increasingly affecting our younger generations? In *The Acid-Alkaline Lifestyle,* best-selling author Larry Trivieri, Jr. and Dr. Neil Raff provide a simple answer to these very important questions.

For decades, physicians and medical researchers have used the body's acid-alkaline balance, or pH level, as a way of determining a patient's overall health status. The problem is that the test most often performed to check acid-alkaline balance—the pH blood test—rarely reveals a shift away from a normal pH reading until acute, life-threatening diseases strike. By then, it is often too late to take action. Left undetected, this corrosive buildup of acid sets the stage for most of the disease conditions that now afflict our nation. Over the years, a number of books have promoted ways to keep acid-alkaline levels in check through diet and nutrition. But to truly achieve and maintain acid-alkaline balance requires far more than a change in diet. *The Acid-Alkaline Lifestyle* presents the first and only complete acid-alkaline balancing program—one that goes far beyond diet and nutrition to include breathing, exercise, and stress relief techniques.

Let *The Acid-Alkaline Lifestyle* guide you in restoring and maintaining your health so you can achieve the long life nature intended.

$17.95 US • 272 pages • 6 x 9-inch quality paperback • ISBN 978-0-7570-0389-9

VICKI'S VEGAN KITCHEN
Eating with Sanity, Compassion & Taste
Vicki Chelf

Vegan dishes are healthy, delicious, and surprisingly easy to make. Yet many people are daunted by the idea of preparing meals that contain no animal products. For them, and for everyone who loves great food, vegetarian chef Vicki Chelf presents *Vicki's Vegan Kitchen,* a comprehensive cookbook designed to take the mystery out of meatless meals.

Whether you're interested in compassionate cooking, you value the benefits of a meat-free diet, or you just want to treat your family to a wonderful meal, this book will bring delectable vegan fare to your kitchen table.

$17.95 • 368 pages • 7.5 x 9-inch quality paperback • ISBN 978-0-7570-0251-9

THE WORLD GOES RAW COOKBOOK
An International Collection of Raw Vegetarian Recipes
Lisa Mann

People everywhere know that meals prepared without heat can taste great and improve their overall health. Yet raw cuisine cookbooks have always offered little variety—until now. In *The World Goes Raw Cookbook,* raw food chef Lisa Mann provides a fresh approach to (un)cooking with recipes that have an international twist.

Whether you are already interested in raw food or are exploring it for the first time, the taste-tempting recipes in *The World Goes Raw* can add variety to your life while helping you feel healthier and more energized.

$16.95 • 194 pages • 7.5 x 9-inch quality paperback • ISBN 978-0-7570-0320-2

EAT SMART, EAT RAW
Creative Vegetarian Recipes for a Healthier Life
Kate Wood

As the popularity of raw vegetarian cuisine continues to soar, so does the mounting scientific evidence that uncooked food is amazingly good for you. From healing diseases to detoxifying your body, from lowering cholesterol to eliminating excess weight, the many important health benefits derived from such a diet are too important to ignore. However, now there is another compelling reason to go raw—taste! In her new book *Eat Smart, Eat Raw*, cook and health writer Kate Wood not only explains how to get started, but also provides delicious kitchen-tested recipes guaranteed to surprise and delight even the fussiest of eaters.

$15.95 US / $21.95 CAN • 184 Pages • 7.5 x 9-inch quality paperback • ISBN 0-7570-0261-7

GOING WILD IN THE KITCHEN
The Fresh & Sassy Tastes of Vegetarian Cooking
Leslie Cerier

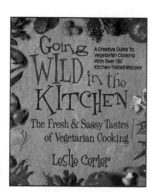

Go wild in the kitchen! Be creative! Venture beyond the usual beans, grains, and vegetables to include an exciting variety of organic vegetarian fare in your meals. Step outside the box and prepare dishes with beautiful edible flowers; flavorful wild mushrooms, herbs, and berries; tangy sheep and goat cheeses; tasty sea vegetables; and exotic ancient grains like teff, quinoa, and Chinese "forbidden" black rice. Author and expert chef Leslie Cerier is crazy about the great taste and goodness of organically grown foods. In this exciting cookbook, she shares scores of her favorite recipes that spotlight these fresh, wholesome ingredients.

$16.95 US / $25.50 CAN • 240 Pages • 7.5 x 9-inch quality paperback • ISBN 0-7570-0091-6

GREENS AND GRAINS
ON THE DEEP BLUE SEA COOKBOOK
Fabulous Vegetarian Cuisine from The Taste of Health Cruises
Sandy Pukel and Mark Hanna

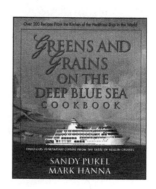

You are invited to come aboard one of America's premier health cruises. Too busy to get away? Well, even if you can't swim in the ship's pool, you can still enjoy its gourmet cuisine, because natural foods expert Sandy Pukel and master chef Mark Hanna have now put together *Greens and Grains on the Deep Blue Sea Cookbook*—a titanic collection
of healthful and delicious vegetarian recipes that are among the most popular dishes served aboard the Taste of Health voyages offered through Costa Cruises.

$18.95 US / $23.95 CAN • 256 Pages • 7.5 x 9-inch quality paperback • ISBN 0-7570-0287-0

GLYCEMIC INDEX FOOD GUIDE

For Weight Loss, Cardiovascular Health, Diabetic Management, and Maximum Energy

Dr. Shari Lieberman

The glycemic index (GI) is an important nutritional tool. By indicating how quickly a given food triggers a rise in blood sugar, the GI enables you to choose foods that can help you manage a variety of conditions, as well as improve your overall health.

Written by Dr. Shari Lieberman, one of America's leading nutritionists, this book was designed as an easy-to-use guide to the glycemic index. The book first looks at commonly asked questions about the GI. What are carbohydrates, and what do they have to do with the GI? How is the GI of a food calculated? What is glycemic load? How are high-GI foods associated with diabetes, obesity, and other health problems? How can a low-GI diet improve your health? The author answers these questions and more, ensuring that you truly understand the index and know how to use it. She then provides both the glycemic index and the glycemic load of hundreds of foods and beverages, including raw foods, cooked foods, and many combination and prepared foods. Throughout, helpful tips guide you towards the best dietary choices.

Whether you are interested in controlling your glucose levels to manage your diabetes, lose weight, increase your heart health, boost your energy level, or simply enhance your well-being, *Glycemic Index Food Guide* is the best place to start.

$7.95 • 160 pages • 4 x 7-inch mass paperback • ISBN 978-0-7570-0245-8